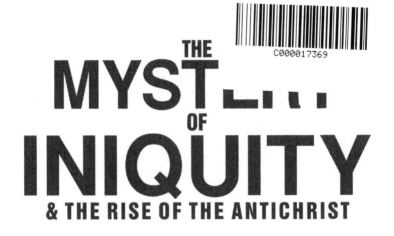

THE
MYSTERY
OF
INIQUITY
& THE RISE OF THE ANTICHRIST

C000017369

TOKUNBO
EMMANUEL

FOREWORD BY DR. HUGH OSGOOD

SOPHOS
SB
BOOKS

The Mystery of Iniquity & The Rise of The Antichrist

Copyright © 2022 by Tokunbo Emmanuel

Published by
Sophos Books Ltd.

London
sophosbooks.com

ISBN 978-1-905669-87-5

Cover illustration and design by *Sophos Books Ltd.*
Printed in the United Kingdom

CONTENTS

To the Alpha and the Omega,
the One who rules over the affairs of man
in every generation.

ENDORSEMENTS

Every once in a long while, you read a book that makes you ask, "Why was this not written earlier?" This book is a clarion call to all about the coming of the Lord. The sad reality is that too many have no clue about the precursors to this great event: The Mystery of Iniquity and the Rise of The Antichrist. The book is well researched, carefully compiled, and prayerfully presented, to make you ready for the greatest meeting yet. Read it carefully, study it prayerfully, and be confident as you wait patiently for Christ's appearing.

Frank Ofosu-Appiah
All Nations Church, Atlanta, GA, USA

Many years ago, as a young Christian, I was 'terrified' by teachings and predictions concerning the end times, especially the rapture, tribulation, and the mark of the beast. To overcome my fears, I convinced myself that end-time events were in God's hands, and He alone knows the *which, what, how* and *when* of their fulfilment. I avoided discussions around the end time, and simply focused on serving God, the best way that He enabled me to.

I am glad, however, that I read *The Mystery of Iniquity!* It is not predictive. Rather, I found it to be *exploratory* and *explanatory*, giving one the scope to carefully reflect on what the scriptures exactly say about the subject. The book is full of insight. It also helps one to consider and understand current events, from a biblical perspective.

After reading *The Mystery of Iniquity*, I concluded that, ultimately, our faith in the sovereignty of God should enable us to trust Him to fulfil His eternal agenda for the last days. In the meantime, we must continue holding on to God and His word, standing in faith, proclaiming the Gospel of the Kingdom, whilst watching and praying, and earnestly awaiting the return of our Lord and Saviour Jesus Christ.

Apostle Jennifer Abigail Lawson-Wallace
President, Women In Tune International, UK

Tokunbo has produced a book that avoids becoming entrenched in philosophical conjecture and allegorical assumptions, by delivering a coherent and spiritual perspective of one of the most crucial and anticipated moments in human history. *The Mystery of Iniquity,* whilst maintaining a sound hermeneutical thread throughout, challenges us to cultivate prophetic pre-ciseness in how we read and apply the scriptures in these challenging times.

Tokunbo reminds us that since the inevitable rise of the Antichrist is not a surprise to an omniscient God, therefore the Scriptures are given to equip us in navigating past the pitfalls of deception and self-governance.

I encourage every believer to have this book as a

resource and a reference to the fact that even though lawlessness is already at work, at the end we win!

Bishop Noel McLean
YCF Network of Churches

If the trumpet gave an uncertain sound, who would prepare himself for battle? The *sound* from this prophetic trumpet is *certain* and its urgent message is clear. If you are concerned about the times we are living in, and your heart longs for the return of our King, then *The Mystery of Iniquity* is a must-read book. My gratitude goes to brother Tokunbo for yielding himself to the Lord and engaging in this noble kingdom task. He who once asked the Church to *run* is now admonishing her to *prepare*.

Oluwole Owolabi
Ergates International Ministry, Nigeria

Every once in a long while, someone picks up the grace to do a work that becomes an instrument for understanding the Scriptures and discerning the mind of God on a matter. Like *Pilgrim's Progress* by John Bunyan, for instance. These works are not mere books; they are tools for discernment; they act as a guide, and they guard; they help us to navigate and explore our faith. Such a book is about to hit the world right now.

The Mystery of Iniquity by Tokunbo Emmanuel is an instrument and a tool for the times we live in. It is not just prophetic, it is practical. It sheds light on many issues and raises many questions about things we thought we knew and understood. This book should drive Christians everywhere to two places: their knees *and* the pages of the Bible.

Elsie Oghenekaro
ElsieWrite Ltd., Nigeria

ACKNOWLEDGEMENTS

Firstly, I am grateful to God, the One whose name is *Alpha*, who inspired, guided, and fashioned this book from beginning to end. I cannot take credit for a work that is entirely the Holy Spirit's.

Thanks to my dear wife, Linda, and youngest child, David, who had to endure months of divided attention at home because I was focused on writing. Destiny and Daniel also spurred me on towards the finish line. Thank you everyone! Your love and support are invaluable.

In 1989, my mother, Pastor Mrs. Esther Olulaja, typed my first manuscript ever, titled *Mysteries of the Kingdom of God*. One of the chapters was *The mystery of iniquity!* Thank you, mum, for the years of unwavering support.

Many thanks to my scribal support group, Mayoress Elsie Oghenekaro, Eyitope Lala, and

Toyin Oladele, for holding my hands in prayer as I wrote.

Special thanks to Dr. Hugh Osgood, who, as always, gave valuable feedback on the manuscript. His depth of insight and fatherly guidance, which have served me for many years, are priceless. Thanks also to my friend, Bishop Noel McLean, for his input on a key section of the book. I was encouraged in no small measure by the thoughts of my long-time friend, Rev. Oluwole Owolabi, and that of Rev. Frank Ofosu-Appiah, Apostle Jennifer Wallace, and John Ingle (thanks, John, for recommending *Raptureless*).

Thanks to everyone who took keen interest in the work and supported its release, including my siblings, cousins, and extended family; everyone in my book launch team; my friends in *The Scribal Hub,* and the *Scribal Prophets* group led by Apostle Theresa Harvard Johnson; my new friends at the *Association of Christian Writers (UK)*; my *ECU Choir* family and the wider *ECU Alumni* fellowship; brethren at the *Wandsworth Council Christian Fellowship*; the *Faith Clinic* family; *The Ark Mission*, my local church family... Truth is, there are too many names to mention in this section!

Finally, I give every praise to the Lord, whose name is *Omega*, the Christ, the Head of the Church, the soon and coming King!

FOREWORD

The rise of lawlessness and the revealing of the son of perdition (the Antichrist) are topics that act as a magnet for some and a deterrent to others. Nonetheless, Paul wrote to Timothy, saying that *"all Scripture is given by inspiration of God and is profitable for doctrine, for reproof, for correction, for instruction in righteousness."* So, we must acknowledge a real debt to those who not only draw us towards less familiar verses, but also cause us to consider them in a wider context. These are the authors who prevent us from being side-tracked, either by our over-caution or by our over-enthusiasm. It would be hard to find a more balanced approach to 2 Thessalonians 2 than that offered here by Tokunbo Emmanuel.

In his introduction, the writer admits he found it daunting to take on a passage with such an 'end-time' significance. He speaks of treading carefully, and he most certainly has done so, but not in a way that leaves us feeling that he is uncertain about the way ahead. He has a clear sense of direction and leads us forward without ever losing sight of the path. This is no minor achievement when he is walking us through areas where conspiracy theories abound, and speculation can fly off at a tangent the moment that it takes leave of the truth.

But this book is much, much more than a lesson on how to walk circumspectly through Scripture. It offers us a valuable guide to unfolding events, and will no doubt prove a helpful handbook for navigating future challenges. Right now, it puts into perspective all that is unfolding around us and that is something that none of us should treat lightly.

Many ask how the Church will endure all that lies ahead. Some are so convinced of the Church's poor durability that they are quick to say that it won't have to endure much at all. Whatever one's point of view, I want to see a Church that is set on being victorious and not just fighting for survival. If you agree with me on this, do keep it in mind as you read this book.

The early chapters of the book of Revelation speak of rewards for seven churches that were urged to set their sights on being overcomers. This book reminds us of the need to set *our* sights with equal determination. It is a call to overcome, and we need to respond to the call. Welcome to the world of better-informed and (hopefully) more effective overcomers.

> *'Now may our Lord Jesus Christ Himself, and our God and Father who has loved us and given us everlasting consolation and good hope by grace, comfort your hearts and establish you in every good word and work.'*
>
> **(2 Thessalonians 2:16-17)**

Dr Hugh Osgood

Charis Communications, UK

AUTHOR'S PREFACE

I embarked on this scribal project about the end times because the Lord bid me to write. I had to step out of the boat of comfort and familiarity, and walk towards Christ, the Word, on the raging sea of world events and popular opinion. Conscious of the boisterous winds of doctrine that were blowing around me from every side, I took one step after the other, fixing my eyes on Christ who stood gloriously before me. Before long, I became terrified by the whirling winds and started to sink. But Jesus lovingly offered His hand, pulled me up, and encouraged my faith. "Do not be afraid. Fix your eyes on me. Keep going. I am here before and beside you. I am the One you seek." I can now testify that it is possible to walk on "water" and not drown. The secret is to focus the eyes and heart on Jesus no matter the rustling of the winds.

This same Jesus is now bidding you to read this book at such a time as this. He might seem at first like a ghost in the gloomy night of end-time uncertainties, but if you can discern the Lord's voice, be assured He will not lead you astray. He prompted you to pick up this book and is by your side as you read. He will not allow you to sink into the troubled waters of global events or get blown away by the winds of theological controversies.

If you do not step out of the boat, you will not experience the miracle and freedom of walking on water. Determine, therefore, to read through to the end and expect to encounter Christ within these pages. With Jesus by your side, you too can remain on top of the troubled sea of end-time drama. At the end, may we, both reader and writer, burst forth in worship, and say, "Truly, You are the Son of God" and the soon coming King! (See Matthew 14:22-33).

INTRODUCTION

The Bible has a lot to say about the end of time or the last days. There are entire books or whole chapters in books that discuss "the end" or events that lead to the end, with numerous pieces of the end-time puzzle scattered throughout God's word - from the multiple visions of Daniel to the discourse of Jesus on the Mount of Olives, to the revelations of John on the Island of Patmos. Students and teachers of the word have, for many years, pondered over these prophetic accounts to comprehend what the Bible teaches about the last days, and to make sense of global events.

Some place happenings in the world alongside prophetic statements to deduce the meaning or highlight the fulfilment of such statements. Others explore prophetic symbolisms and use them to dissect history or predict the world's destiny. Consequently, we now have various schools of eschatological opinions and understanding—"eschatology" being a branch of theology that studies "last things" or "end things," in this case the final destiny of the world, humanity, and the angelic order as revealed in scripture. Directly or indirectly, as an individual believer, you have been influenced by one or a combination of these theological perspectives.

The primary aim of this book is *not* to answer every eschatological question; it is also *not* to resolve every theological bottleneck or work out which perspective is right, and which is wrong. Instead, the book seeks to contribute meaningfully to this ever-growing body of end-time prophetic commentary. Its aim is to provide a few pieces of the end-time puzzle—*one* in particular—and enhance the comprehension of what the reader already knows (or wants to know). As these truths become evident (and hopefully they will as the reading progresses), I trust that the Holy Spirit will highlight present-day applications in their various forms.

APPROACHES TO ESCHATOLOGICAL STUDIES

There are, seemingly, different approaches to the exploration or study of Bible prophecies about the last days. Some of these approaches include the following:

Prophetic Timeline approach

There are prophecies in the Bible that state the duration or give a time stamp for some events (for example, "And *from the time that the daily sacrifice* is taken away, and the abomination of desolation is set up, there shall be *one thousand two hundred and ninety days*" - Daniel 12:11). Some scholars delve into these prophetic time-lines, the days and the weeks, and align them with historical events to understand their meaning and project into the future.

Empire Prominence approach

The Bible records prophecies about the rise and fall of many global kingdoms, from the global era of ancient Babylon right up to the end of time (for example, Daniel's interpretation of Nebuchadnezzar's dreams - Daniel 2:27-45). This approach focuses on comprehending the succession of these kingdoms and how they relate to the end of time.

End-time Signs approach

Jesus predicted the manifestation of some signs that will point to the time of the end (for example, wars, earthquakes, famines, etc. - Matthew 24:6-8). Some examine these signs as they occur to comprehend and interpret prophetic end-time events.

Fig Tree Sign approach

When Jesus said we should gain insight from observing the "Fig tree," some take this as a reference to the nation of Israel. These scholars take a keen interest in prophecies about Israel, and what is going on in modern-day Israel and the Middle East as a whole (Matthew 24:32-33).

The Endgame approach

God declares the end from the beginning, and the Bible, severally, predicts things that would happen at the end of time (for example, the second coming Christ; the devil's eternal judgement in the lake of fire; the emergence of a new heaven and new earth, etc.). Exploring these endgame themes in scripture and how they will come about is another approach to studying end-time teachings.

Tribulation Theory approach

The Bible alludes to a period of severe suffering that will befall inhabitants of the earth (see Matthew 24:21 for example), especially at the hand of a world ruler. How and when this will happen, and whether it will occur before or after the coming of Christ are some of the key contentions of this approach.

Millennium Theory approach

The Bible also makes mention of a thousand-year reign of Christ on the earth, during which the devil will be bound in chains (Revelation 20:2-3,5). What this entails and *when* it will materialise—before or after Christ's second coming—is another approach to exploring end-time prophecies.

Bible Exposition approach

There are entire sections of the Bible that contextually discuss end of time events (for example, the teachings of Christ in Matthew 24). A thorough hermeneutic exploration of these texts is also a common approach to understanding the end times.

THIS BOOK'S APPROACH

All these approaches to studying the last days have their merits, and in many ways, they are all intertwined. No single approach nullifies the others and none, perhaps, exclusively gives a complete picture. Yet, there is value in exploring the subject from one viewpoint and, where there are overlaps, gaining insight from other approaches.

This book seeks to comprehend the events of the last days using a *Bible Exposition approach,* and the primary text it will explore is Paul's message to the Thessalonian believers recorded in 2 Thessalonians 2. At the least, exploring an entire text of Scripture should add to the reader's understanding of the text itself and the biblical theme it discusses. It should, I hope, also create a hunger for God's word in the reader and birth a desire to rightly divide God's word. In exploring this text, therefore, we would largely allow scripture to explain scripture.

A VITAL KEY

There is a vital key within this text that could, I believe, help us understand end-time theology a bit more from a practical and relatable stand-point. The moment you *see* this concept and grasp its significance, you will not only appreciate the authenticity of Bible prophecy and recognise how end-time predictions are unfolding today; you will also be motivated to fight a good fight of faith to the very end. The vital key in this text, as the title of the book suggests, is *The Mystery of Iniquity.* What is this mystery all about? What is its role in the culmination of end-time prophecy? Why is it important for your understanding of the last days? You are about to discover answers to these questions.

As noted above, all the end-time study approaches overlap in some way. So, there would be references made to some derivations from other viewpoints. The goal is not to simply repeat the explorative arguments of other studies, but to properly expound on this Pauline letter and consider how it fits with the wider body of eschatological understanding. We will start from the first verse of our text and build the necessary context around this important epistle.

BEWARE YOUR ESCHATOLOGICAL GOGGLES!

Inevitably, depending on your denominational affiliation or spiritual developmental background, you probably have already formed some conviction about Bible prophecy and end-time events. For example, you might hold a position about *when* Jesus will return and when the Church will be gathered unto Him. Interestingly, some people do not hold any view at all! Asked to describe their position about when Christ would come, *before* or *after* the Great Tribulation, 14.6% of respondents to my survey said they were not sure![1]

However, as is usually the case when end-time prophecies are discussed, your position might come into question as you read, or you might question a position that the book seems to present. The primary aim of this work, as earlier stated, is *not* to present, prove, or disprove any theological conclusion, neither is it to solve every eschatological conundrum, but to explore a portion of scripture in its context and explain the *vital key* that could unlock present-day understanding of end-time events. Every other thing is consequential. So, at the least, be aware of your eschatological bias, and be prepared to lay them aside for a while to engage, as objectively as possible, with the insights the book is presenting.

You do not have to agree with all that is written herein. However, I stress this point for you not to miss, or subconsciously overlook, because of preconceived notions, the numerous revelations from God's word that are scattered throughout the book.

As you step out of your theological boat and unto these waters of knowledge and events, keep your eyes on Jesus Christ, "the pioneer and perfecter of our faith" (Hebrews 12:2 RSV). As the *pioneer of faith,* Jesus, through the word and the Spirit, births understanding in us sufficient for the exercise of saving faith. As the *perfecter of faith*, He, again through the word and the Spirit, births understanding in us sufficient for an increasingly mature walk of faith. If you are already saved, it is expected that the things you comprehend about God and His word today are richer and deeper than what you knew when you first believed.[2] (If you are not yet saved, may you find saving faith through the reading of this book!).

The entrance and unfolding of God's word gives light and understanding. May the truths of God come to life in you as you read this book. May your path in these last and evil days become brighter as revelation knowledge floods your heart. Amen.

THE TEXT

2 THESSALONIANS 2:1-17

¹ Now, brethren, concerning the coming of our Lord Jesus Christ and our gathering together to Him, we ask you,

² not to be soon shaken in mind or troubled, either by spirit or by word or by letter, as if from us, as though the day of Christ had come.

³ Let no one deceive you by any means; for that Day will not come unless the falling away comes first, and the man of sin is revealed, the son of perdition,

⁴ who opposes and exalts himself above all that is called God or that is worshiped, so that he sits as God in the temple of God, showing himself that he is God.

⁵ Do you not remember that when I was still with you I told you these things?

⁶ And now you know what is restraining, that he may be revealed in his own time.

⁷ For the mystery of lawlessness is already at work; only He who now restrains will do so until He is taken out of the way.

⁸ And then the lawless one will be revealed, whom the Lord will consume with the breath of His mouth and destroy with the brightness of His coming.

⁹ *The coming of the lawless one is according to the working of Satan, with all power, signs, and lying wonders,*

¹⁰ *and with all unrighteous deception among those who perish, because they did not receive the love of the truth, that they might be saved.*

¹¹ *And for this reason God will send them strong delusion, that they should believe the lie,*

¹² *that they all may be condemned who did not believe the truth but had pleasure in unrighteousness.*

¹³ *But we are bound to give thanks to God always for you, brethren beloved by the Lord, because God from the beginning chose you for salvation through sanctification by the Spirit and belief in the truth,*

¹⁴ *to which He called you by our gospel, for the obtaining of the glory of our Lord Jesus Christ.*

¹⁵ *Therefore, brethren, stand fast and hold the traditions which you were taught, whether by word or our epistle.*

¹⁶ *Now may our Lord Jesus Christ Himself, and our God and Father, who has loved us and given us everlasting consolation and good hope by grace,*

¹⁷ *comfort your hearts and establish you in every good word and work.*

1

CONCERNING THE COMING OF OUR LORD JESUS CHRIST

P aul, in the portion of his epistle that we want to explore, clearly stated the theme and purpose of his letter to the Thessalonians. He wrote to them "concerning the coming of our Lord Jesus Christ and our gathering to Him," and it was important that he did so because some were saying that Christ had *already* come. We will first explore this theme of Christ's second coming and, thereafter, take note of Paul's apostolic responsibility to refute these false claims.

CHRIST'S SECOND COMING

The second coming of Christ is a major event in Christian eschatology. It is the focal point of many views on the end times: the *fact* of His coming; what will happen *before* and *after* He comes; the *manner* of His coming; the *timing* of His coming. It is also an anchor of our faith because the fact of Christ's second coming *and* the resurrection of the saints that will occur when He comes are assurances of our eternal future in God's Kingdom. For "if in this life only we have hope in Christ, we are of all men most pitiable" (1 Corinthians 15:19).

Notice how Paul named both events as themes of his letter: "Concerning the coming of our Lord Jesus Christ *and* our gathering together to Him." In other words, when Jesus comes again, there will be a gathering together to meet Him. These two events, it seems, are distinct, sequential, and inseparable. They are cornerstones of all the prophecies about the last days.

Jesus Himself said it clearly, that He will not only come again, but also gather the saints to Himself when He comes.

> "Let not your heart be troubled; you believe in God, believe also in Me. In My Father's house are many mansions; if it were not so, I would have told you. I go to prepare a place for you. And if I go and prepare a place for you, **I will come again and receive you to Myself;** that where I am, there you may be also."
>
> **(John 14:1-3)**

The two angels who were eyewitnesses of Christ's ascension said to the disciples standing by, "Men of Galilee, why do you stand gazing up into heaven? *This same Jesus,* who was taken up from you into heaven, *will so come in like manner* as you saw Him go into heaven" (Acts 1:11).

Paul also wrote the following in his first letter to the Thessalonians:

> *"For this we say to you by the word of the Lord, that we who are alive and remain **until the coming of the Lord** will by no means precede those who are asleep. **For the Lord Himself will descend** from heaven with a shout, with the voice of an archangel, and with the trumpet of God. **And the dead in Christ will rise first. Then we who are alive and remain shall be caught up together with them in the clouds to meet the Lord in the air.** And thus we shall always be with the Lord."*
>
> **(I Thessalonians 4:15-17)**

These are, indeed, words of comfort and hope for believers of every age. There should be no ambiguity about this truth, that the Lord is coming and will come. Jesus alluded to His coming in many of His parables and spoke the words of the book of Revelation to John.

> *"Behold, **He is coming with clouds**, and every eye will see Him, even they who pierced Him. And all the tribes of the earth will mourn*

because of Him. Even so, Amen."

(Revelation 1:7)

Severally, in this prophetic revelation, Jesus said, "I am coming soon" (Revelation 22:7,12,20 NIV). Blessed are all who look forward to and long for His appearing.

LET NOT YOUR HEART BE TROUBLED

Apart from wanting to teach the believers about the second coming of Christ, Paul wrote this epistle to calm the hearts and minds of the saints because some were spreading false teachings that Christ had *already come.* He countered this misinformation and encouraged them "not to be soon shaken in mind or troubled either by spirit or by word or by letter" (2 Thessalonians 2:2).

There are crucial times in the life of a congregation when those in spiritual leadership need to confront error and protect the saints with truth. How can some say that Christ had already come? In Paul's day, there were those who promoted teachings that denied the coming of Christ in the flesh. *Gnostics*[1], for instance, disputed the incarnation of Christ, saying that there was no way deity could take on mortality. The truth about Christ's incarnation, however, is foundational to the new covenant and our salvation: "the Word *became* flesh and dwelt among us" (John 1:14). Indeed, "without controversy great is the mystery of godliness: *God was manifested in the flesh*" (1 Timothy 3:15).

By denying the first coming of Christ *in the flesh*, this erroneous teaching consequently denied His second coming "in the flesh." Proponents of this error taught that Christ had already come in some spiritual or figurative sense, supposedly causing enlightenment or heightened consciousness. These doctrines unsettled the believers, more so that some of the false teachers claimed that Paul taught the same thing. For this reason, Paul put the record straight. One, he never taught or wrote such things - they are not "from us". And two, Christ had *not* yet come.

These kinds of doctrines still exist today in different forms. Gnostic teachings have found their way into popular Christianity, and it takes spiritual discernment to weed out the errors. However, as pertaining to the end of time prophecies, Christ has not yet come. When He comes, all eyes shall see Him. He will come "in like manner" as His ascension. He is coming literally and not figuratively.

There are also those who mock that Christ is no longer coming. "Where is the promise of His coming?" they say. "All things continue as they were from the beginning of creation," they scoff (2 Peter 3:4). These also can unsettle the heart and throw believers into confusion. But we need to remain immovable in our convictions. Our hearts need to remain untroubled.

Another reason why believers need to guard their hearts against anxiety is the impact of tribulation in the world. The apprehension and uncertainty that accompany end-time events call for such counsel. Aware of all the shakings that would happen before and after His death and resurrection, Jesus not only gave assurances about His second coming; He also told the disciples: "Let not your heart be troubled" (John 14:1). Throughout the ages, when oppressive governments wreak havoc or when natural disasters occur, people instinctively tend to make references to end-time prophecies and wonder whether they are witnessing their fulfilment. Over-analysing and focusing on these events can throw the uninformed into confusion. There are many scary things happening in our world today that can unsettle the fainthearted. As God's people, we need to remain untroubled in heart.

Moreover, there is an eschatological viewpoint today, the *preterist*[1] viewpoint, that believes the prophecies of the Bible have come to pass already. Proponents of this theory postulate that either *most* of the prophecies (partial preterism) or *all* end-time prophecies (full preterism) have been fulfilled. Preterists give particular attention to the discourse of Christ in Matthew 24 (also recorded in Mark 13 and Luke 21) and relate it exclusively to the destruction of the temple in Jerusalem, which happened in AD 70. They teach that Jesus had *already* come to judge Jerusalem, which was His answer to the disciples' questions: "Tell us, when will *these things* be," referring to the destruction of the second temple in Jerusalem; "What would be the *sign of your coming*, and of the *end of the age*?" (Matthew 24:3). Full preterists say there is no further advent of Christ, whilst partial preterists expect Christ to come again in the future as ruler over God's righteous kingdom.

For us to withstand these theological storms, the shakings around the globe, and the uncertainties of end-time events, we need a solid foundation in the truths of God's word. Church leaders also need to settle the minds of the believers and teach these truths.

Paul considered it important to write to the believers when some claimed that Christ had already come. Peter thought it necessary to write to the saints when others mocked that Christ would no longer come. Jesus our Lord gave John the mandate to write His message to the churches, admonishing that He would return soon. Therefore, in times like these, we must "not be soon shaken in mind or troubled, either by spirit or by word or by letter." Instead, we should encourage one another to stand firm in faith no matter what befalls the world, knowing that we are not in the dark regarding the times and seasons of Christ's return. This is what Paul goes on to discuss next.

2

THAT DAY WILL NOT COME UNLESS...

By refuting the claim that Christ had already come, Paul invariably implied that the Lord's second coming would happen in the future. However, if he had only rebutted the assertion and not given some indication about *when* Christ would return, an air of curiosity would have remained over the believers. This same kind of curiosity is what led the disciples to ask Jesus privately, "Tell us, when will these things be? And what will be the sign of Your coming, and of the end of the age?" (Matthew 24:3). Jesus had predicted the future destruction of the temple in Jerusalem, hence the questions. The truth is, people are always keen to know what could happen in the future, and believers are asking similar questions today!

As we noted in the introduction, one of the approaches scholars have used to analyse end of time prophecies is the *Timeline Approach*, which attempts to answer the "when" question of end-time prophetic events. They take scriptures like Daniel 9:24-27, Daniel 12:11-12, Revelation 11:2-3, and many others, scriptures that have chronological time stamps (days, weeks, months, years), and use them to either confirm the fulfilment of prophecy or predict when yet-to-be-fulfilled prophecies are likely to come to pass.

Some of the milestone points of interest in the *Timeline Approach* include the destruction of Jerusalem in AD 70, the reconstitution of Israel as a nation in 1948, both being past events; the second coming of Christ and the resurrection of the saints, both future events. If history affirms the authenticity of Bible prophecy, we have every reason to expect the fulfilment of every yet-to-be-fulfilled prophecy. Moreover, providing we avoid the trap of date-setting or date-suggesting, there is a place for exploring the season or signs of Christ's coming alongside other events. We can observe the signs, but we should not set dates because Jesus said clearly that only the Father knows the *time*, the exact "day and hour" of His coming (Matthew 24:36).

In the New Testament, there are a few Greek words that are translated as *time*. The word *chronos* refers to a space or passage of time (measured in years, months, and days). *Kairos* denotes a definite time or a season of opportunity for a thing to occur. *Hora,* another Greek word for time, refers to a specific or an appropriate time. Relating these to Christ's second coming, only the Father knows the exact timing of His appearance. It is not for us "to know the *kairos* or *chronos* which the Father has put in His own authority" (Acts 1:7). Yet, He does not want us to be ignorant of the opportunity that the times presents to us to be prepared for His coming. We should, like the sons of Issachar, understand the times and respond accordingly (see 1 Chronicles 12:32).

Herein lies the usefulness and limitation of the *Timeline Approach* to comprehending end-time prophecies. We should not dabble into predicting the date of Christ's return, nor should we entertain anyone who does, no matter their status. Yet, we should understand the signs of His coming and the events that should happen before He returns. Paul demonstrated such an understanding.

THE PAULINE TIMELINE OF CHRIST'S RETURN

So, how did Paul address the question of *when* Christ would return? He made this emphatic statement: "That Day will not come *unless* the falling away comes *first*, and the man of sin is revealed" (2 Thessalonians 2:3). In other words, from a *kairos* timeline perspective, an opportune time, Christ's second coming would be preceded by "the falling away," which must come *first*, and the revealing of the man of sin (see the diagram below).

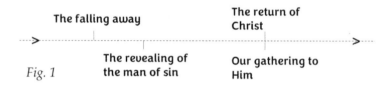

Fig. 1

There are, according to the scriptures, some events that would take place *before* Christ returns, including the preaching of the gospel of the Kingdom to the ends of the earth (Matthew 24:14) and the restoration of all things (Acts 3:20-21). I wrote about some of these in my book, *Run Church Run,* in the chapter titled *"When would Jesus stand up from His throne?"* However, in keeping with the exposition of our main text, we will focus on the events Paul specifically mentioned: *the falling away* and *the revealing of the man of sin* (we will examine these two phenomena in chapters 6 and 7).

The falling away and the revealing of the man of sin seem to be interconnected situations. Both, according to Paul, would happen *before* Christ returns. The former will lead to the latter. The falling away will pave the way for the revealing of the man of sin, and until *both* occurrences fully manifest, Christ would not return.

WHAT ABOUT THE GREAT TRIBULATION?

Although not the primary focus of this study, an in-depth exploration of this statement of Paul inevitably leads to the tribulation theories about Christ's second coming. These theories attempt to explain the timing of Christ's second coming *vis a vis* the rise of The Antichrist, the gathering of the saints, the Great Tribulation, and the millennial reign of Christ. What is the order of these end-time events? Will the church witness or avoid the Great Tribulation?

First, it is worth mentioning that the phrase "Great Tribulation" was used only by Christ when He taught His disciples prophetically about the destruction of the Jewish temple and the end of time (see Matthew 24:21). As a cross reference, Jesus also mentioned "the 'abomination of desolation,' spoken of by Daniel the prophet" (Matthew 24:15, see also Daniel 9:27, 11:31, 12:11). The idea of a seven-year treaty made with Israel is derived from this Daniel reference ("Then he shall confirm a covenant with many for *one week...*" a day representing one year). The other references to the phrase "Great

Tribulation" are in Revelation 2:22, where Jesus said He will cast the church in Thyatira *into* great tribulation, and Revelation 7:14, referring to "a great multitude which no one could number... who *come out* of the great tribulation."

There are ongoing debates as to whether Christ's reference to a Great Tribulation is limited to the AD 70 destruction of Jerusalem and the severe adversity that occurred during that time (the preterist view) or whether there are parallel periods of tribulation that will still occur. Evidently, there have been many times of devastation since AD 70, and with the emergence of Israel as a nation, threats of more loom in the background. The mass slaughter of six million Jews during the second world war is a telling reminder of the kind of tribulation that can befall a race or a region. If the Antichrist is still to come, then, according to God's word, a period of tribulation is also in the waiting.

Already, we have seen a bird's eye view, based on what Paul has written so far, of the order of these pivotal events — the coming of the Antichrist and the coming of Christ (see fig. 1 on page 42). However, considering a few scriptures, particularly in Daniel, Revelation, and the Gospels, the various viewpoints on the *order* of these events attempt to fit the following events in and around the timeline:

- The seven-year treaty with Israel (Daniel 9:27a).

- The breaking of the treaty and unveiling of the Antichrist (Daniel 9:27b).

- The great tribulation (Matthew 24:21).

- The outpouring of God's wrath on the earth (Revelation 6:16-17).

- The binding of Satan and the millennial reign of Christ on the earth (Revelation 20:1-3).

- The emergence of the New Jerusalem (Revelation 21:1).

A summary of the main theories is as follows:

Pre-tribulation gathering: The second coming of Christ and the gathering of the saints happen *before* the great tribulation.

Mid-tribulation gathering: The second coming and the gathering of the saints happen *midway* into the seven-year treaty, after the Antichrist moves to make things unbearable.

Post-tribulation gathering: The second coming of Christ and the gathering of the saints happen *after* the great tribulation.

Pre-wrath gathering: The second coming of Christ and the gathering of the saints happen *before* the outpouring of God's wrath on the earth.

Pre-millennialism: The thousand-year reign of Christ on the earth happens *after* the literal second coming of Christ on the earth and the gathering of the saints.

Post-millennialism: The thousand-year reign of Christ on the earth happens *before* the second coming of Christ and the gathering of the saints.

So, which ones are right and which ones are wrong? Let us first focus on the commonalities.

- Generally, none of the theories claim that Christ has *already* come physically to earth, which is the error Paul was confronting in his epistle.

- All of the theories affirm that Christ is coming and the saints will be gathered to Him.

- All of the theories advocate for believers to be ready for the Lord's return.

For the sake of this study, we will not embark on an exercise to prove the *correctness* of one position over another. We will, instead, continue to focus on the exposition of Paul's letter, and emphasise the need for *readiness*. Surely, there is a place for studying and dividing God's word *correctly*. There is also a need to live in the light of the convictions we have. As the prophetic word of God continues to unfold, we need to be *ready* for whatever occurs (see *Appendix 2* for tips on how to reconcile eschatological differences).

ARE WE THERE YET?

Going back to Paul's timeline, the twin events that will precede this Christ's coming are *the falling away* and *the revealing of the man of sin*. The day of Christ will not come *until* these two fully play out before our eyes. So, if you are looking for landmarks or signs to determine how close we are to the Lord's coming, these two facts are significant.

According to Christ, there is a place for observing the signs that lead to His coming. There are some signs that inform us that the end is still *far off* (Matthew 24:8), and there are others that signify we are *close* to the end (Matthew 24:33). The falling away and the rise of The Antichrist are sure signs that the coming of Christ is imminent.

If we ask the question, "Whose appearance are we going to see *first*, that of Jesus, the Christ, or the Antichrist?" from our studies so far, it has to be the Antichrist, the man of sin - "for that Day (the coming of Christ) will *not* come *unless...* the man of sin is revealed." The Antichrist, according to Paul's epistle, will come *before* Christ returns. This, perhaps, would be a revelation or a shock to those who have always believed otherwise (more than half of the respondents to my survey, 54.6%, hold a pre-tribulation view). In other words, the Antichrist will come and *then* the Christ, and once the Antichrist is unveiled, we can be sure that the return of our Lord and Christ will soon occur.

This leads us to another question: *When* would the Antichrist be revealed? Asked in another way, how close are we to the unveiling of the man of sin? Paul gave a major clue that points to the emergence of this person. Once we see and comprehend this clue, we will know without a doubt that the end is drawing near. He called this vital detail *the mystery of iniquity*, the secret that would propel the Antichrist to power. However, before Paul talked about this mystery, he said something was holding the Antichrist back. What is this *something*? What is restraining his emergence to the world scene? This is what we will explore next.

3

WHAT IS HOLDING HIM BACK?

We have noted how emphatic Paul was in his assertion about the coming of Christ; that the Antichrist will be revealed *before* Christ returns. In other words, Christ will *not* come until the Antichrist comes to global prominence. However, Paul went on to make a statement that scholars have tried to comprehend and interpret for centuries. He wrote the following to the Thessalonians:

> "And now you know **what is restraining**, that he may be revealed in his own time... **He who now restrains** will do so **until** He is taken out of the way."
>
> ### *(2 Thessalonians 2:6-7)*

Paul added that once this *restraint* is relaxed or removed, "*then* the lawless one would be revealed" (2 Thessalonians 2:8a). What did Paul mean in these verses? Was he implying that something or someone is restraining the unveiling of the Antichrist? If this were so, what or who was Paul referring to?

RESTRAINING EVIL

Before we identify who or what is restraining the unveiling of the Antichrist, let us first explore the concept of restraining evil. To *restrain* means "to prevent someone or something from doing something; to keep under control or within limits." The Greek word, *katecho*, means "to hold fast or down." As long as a restraint is in place, whatever is being restrained would not be able to go beyond the limits imposed on it, even if it wants or attempts to. Presumably, the person or thing that is restraining would need to have greater power or authority compared to the one or thing under restraint, otherwise, the restraint would not last too long.

Applying this definition to the idea of restraining evil, Paul is claiming that something is holding back the full manifestation of lawlessness in the earth. Now, is there any evidence, parallel, or instance in Scripture that can help us understand what this restraint is all about? Apparently, there is. Let us identify a few.

In the days of Noah, the Lord looked at His

creation and "saw that the wickedness of man was *great* in the earth, and that every intent of the thoughts of his heart was only evil continually" (Genesis 6:5). As mankind multiplied on the face of the earth, so did evil. Despite this multiplication of evil, God's Spirit was present on the earth, striving with man and restraining evil's complete manifestation. Owing to the way evil was advancing, God said that *His Spirit* shall not strive or contend with man forever, and He decided to limit man's lifespan to a hundred and twenty years (Genesis 6:3). This reveals one of the roles of the Holy Spirit in the earth, which is to prevent the perpetual showing of wickedness. He is not abiding with man passively but is active in holding evil back.

In the story of Job, the *instruction* and *authority* of God prevented the devil from going beyond the affliction of Job's body and confiscation of his wealth. Even if the devil wanted to, he could not go beyond the limits God placed on him. The word that God spoke was enough to restrain him (see Job 1:12, 2:6).

In both instances, God was the One restraining, and the one being restrained was the devil and the manifestation of his evil works. Without His overruling control, the devil would have operated mercilessly without any boundaries.

RESTRAINING THE ANTICHRIST

Considering these parallels, we can begin to deduce what Paul meant by "He who restrains." He used the neuter *He*, implying that the One who is restraining is a person. This person or personality must be superior in power and authority to the Antichrist that is being restrained. By deduction, this Person would be the Holy Spirit, the One who has been active in the earth since the beginning of creation and more so since His outpouring on the day of Pentecost. Jesus used the same "He" neuter when He talked to His disciples about the Holy Spirit (see John 14:26, 15:26, 16:13-15).

Restraining the full manifestation of lawlessness in the earth seems to be one of the unspoken ministries of the Spirit of God. He convicts "the world of sin, and of righteousness, and of judgment" (John 16:8). He ruminates over the void and darkness of the earth and causes the light of God to shine forth, a shining that darkness cannot overcome.

In practice, the Holy Spirit can accomplish this restraint through various means. Paul used the neuter "He" ("*He* who now restrains"), referring to God through His Spirit, and the pronoun "what" ("you know *what* is restraining"), referring to the *instrument of restraint*. In the days of Noah, the instrument of restraint was death, the cutting short of man's lifespan, as well as the flood. During Job's ordeal, the instrument of restraint was God's express command to the devil. There are some other parallels in Scripture that mirror this concept of an *instrument of restraint*. For instance, during the lifetime of some prophets, the king they served walked in the ways of the Lord. But after the death of the prophet, the king reverted to evil deeds. The existence and presence of the prophet was a restraint preventing the king from indulging in evil. Laban would have harmed Jacob, but the instruction God gave him in a dream restrained him. Also, the governments of the earth are "God's ministers" for the restraint of evildoers (see Romans 13:3-4).

Attempts to understand what instrument of restraint Paul was referring to has led scholars to a variety of conclusions. Suggestions include the Church, the gospel, the Roman empire, governments, the Jews, etc. Is there any justification for these suggestions? Not if they are being put forward as the sole or only restraint. God's Spirit is the One who restrains, but He can employ, in practical terms, agents or mediums of restraint as He wills. For instance, the church in the earth is certainly a force for restraining lawlessness. Whenever the church is strong in the authority of God, the agenda of the devil is always pushed back. Past and present stories of revival are evidence of the role of the Holy Spirit through the Church in standing against evil and pushing back hell's advance. As the light and salt of the earth, the church is an instrument of the Holy Spirit for promoting righteousness and restraining wickedness. Of course, the situation is different if the salt loses its saltiness. God has also used human governments in the past to advance His purpose and prevent evil.

Whichever way the Holy Spirit has employed throughout history to restrain the manifestation of lawlessness in the world, He remains the constant restraining force, whether in the background or foreground. He will continue His ministry of restraining evil *until* the time of the end when the Antichrist is unveiled.

TAKEN OUT OF THE WAY?

Now, if the Holy Spirit is the One restraining the complete evolution of lawlessness in the earth, what did Paul mean when He said the restraint will continue "until He is *taken out of the way*" (2 Thessalonians 2:7)? Does this mean that the Holy Spirit would have to leave the earth for the Antichrist to take control of the world's affairs? Some have used this verse to argue a case for a pre-tribulation rapture of the church. This position claims that the church, being the main agent of restraint, *and* the Holy Spirit, the One who restrains through the church, will both leave the earth (be taken out of the way) before the Antichrist is unveiled.

At times, the presentation of this position portrays the church as needing to *escape* the tribulation that the Antichrist will unleash upon mankind. It promotes an escapist mindset and denies the power that works in the church, the same power that worked in Christ when God raised Him from the dead and positioned Him "above all principality and power and might and dominion, and every name that is named, not only in this age but also in that which is to come" (Ephesians 1:20-21). The church has endured multiple tribulations in the past and emerged victoriously. The scriptures and church history do not support an escapist mindset.

Moreover, the idea that the Holy Spirit will be "taken out" of the earth for evil to permeate humanity is questionable. Would God have to become less omnipresent because of the Antichrist and his lawless era? The rise of the Antichrist is not a case of evil finally overpowering good either. God is forever omnipotent, omniscient, sovereign, and almighty.

Let us read this verse in context. Paul said the coming of Christ will *not* happen *before* the unveiling of the Antichrist and the falling away.

That is, Christ will come *after* the Antichrist is unveiled. So, how can the church be taken from the earth for the Antichrist to appear without the coming of Christ? That is, how can Christ return to take His bride when Paul said categorically that His coming would occur *after* the Antichrist is revealed?

This time "conflict" has led some to put forward a two-phased (or multiple-phased) coming of Christ. The first phase of the second coming of Christ, it is said, would be the rapture of the Church (or the rapture of "true" believers), and the second phase of His coming would be for defeating of the Antichrist. Because of this teaching, believers are enjoined to do everything they can to be found worthy of this first rapture or they would have to go through the ordeal of enduring the Antichrist's regime.

Historically, this doctrine about a catching up of believers *before* the Antichrist regime was not taught by the apostles or the early church fathers. There is no trace or evidence of this teaching in any of the apostolic writings. The doctrine found its way into Christian eschatology as late as the 18th century, through the teachings and writings of scholars like John Darby, C.I. Scofield (author of the *Scofield Reference Bible*), Finis Dake (author of *Dake's Annotated Reference Bible*). These perspectives were further popularised by bestselling books like *The Late Great Planet Earth*, by Hal Lindsay, *Left Behind*, by Tim Lahaye, and other similar media presentations.

It is worth repeating that we need to be *ready* for when Christ returns. It is also important to *rightly* divide God's word and embrace truth in its proper context. When it comes to issues of interpreting prophecy, particularly end-of-time prophecies, the absolutes must remain, which are the return of Christ, the gathering of the saints, and the judgement of evil. On the finer details, we can position ourselves better as we see further light from God's word.

THE ANTICHRIST'S TIME

There is one more statement Paul made about the restraining of lawlessness that we cannot over-look. This statement, in many ways, resolves a lot of uncertainty and debate around the unveiling of the Antichrist and what is holding him back. Paul said that the restraint is in place so that the man of sin can "be revealed *in his own time*" (2 Thessalonians 2:6). In other words, until the *opportune* time, the *Kairos*, for the Antichrist to mount the centre stage, the restraint would remain active.

Who determines this appointed time? It is no other than the almighty God, the One who declares the end from the beginning. He has set a time when the restraining ministry of the Holy Spirit would recede, and the Antichrist would fully manifest to do all that is written concerning his rule. Despite the upsurge of lawlessness in the world, God would remain in control because the devil would know "that he has a *short time*" (Revelation 12:12).

Although it is not for us to know the day or hour that the Father has put in his own authority, He will not leave us in the dark. He will help us understand the signs of the time and prepare for what is to come. There is indeed a vital key that would help us to recognise the times we are in. Paul mentions this key in between the two references to the restraints. He referred to the "mystery of iniquity," a vital piece of the puzzle to knowing what time we are living in.

4

THE MYSTERY OF INIQUITY

In the previous chapters, we have seen how Paul, through his epistle, urged the saints in Thessalonica to remain unruffled by claims that Christ had already returned. The assertion was false because *before* Christ returns, the Antichrist, the man of sin, would be revealed. This person had not yet been made manifest, so the coming of Christ was still to come. Paul also wrote that there was a restraining power that stood in the way of the Antichrist and until this restraint steps aside, the rise of lawlessness will continue to be curtailed. The One who is restraining the elevation of evil is the Holy Spirit, whose ministry it is to prevent its culmination until the *time* the Father has set by His own authority, using any instrument or number of instruments He deems fit.

Paul then gave a telling clue about how the man of sin would establish the coming era of lawlessness. Although the Antichrist's time had not yet matured, there was a secret phenomenon at work that would one day lead to his manifestation. This mystery was already active in the background, and it was only a matter of time before it accomplished its mission of enabling the man of sin. This is how Paul put it:

> *And now you know what is restraining, that he may be revealed in his own time.* **For the mystery of lawlessness is already at work;** *only He who now restrains will do so until He is taken out of the way.*
>
> ### *(2 Thessalonians 2:6-7)*

In other words, the coming era of the man of sin is actively being facilitated by a secret operation, one that is being restrained until the time of the end. This mystery is aggressively preparing for the unveiling of the Antichrist. If it were not for the restraints God put in place, this mystery would have accomplished its objective of ushering in the Antichrist. But the mystery is currently working and will continue to work until lawlessness is fully entrenched in the world.

MYSTERIES IN THE BIBLE

The Greek word *Musterion,* translated *mystery* in the New Testament, means "that which is known only to the initiated." It refers to truth revealed to those who are enlightened by God's Spirit. Jesus, explaining the reason why, many times, He spoke in parables, said "Because it has been given to you *to know the mysteries of the kingdom of heaven*, but to them it has not been given" (Matthew 13:11). In other words, there are truths about the dynamics of God's kingdom that only the saints can comprehend. These truths will remain a secret to the unsaved because "the natural man does not receive the things of the Spirit of God... nor can he know them because they are spiritually discerned" (1 Corinthians 2:14).

For example, there are revealed truths (mysteries) about Christ's love for and union with the church (Ephesians 5:22), the current state of unbelief in Israel (Romans 11:25), and the coming resurrection of the dead (1 Corinthians 15:51), to name a few. So, when Paul referred to "the mystery of iniquity," he was alluding to the *truth* behind the manifestation of lawlessness, insight that should be plain to the believer enlightened by God. In other words, there is something responsible for iniquity and this thing will one day culminate in widespread lawless-ness championed by the man of sin, the Anti-christ. Once we understand what this mystery is and how it operates, we will see clearly how the systems of this world are preparing for the coming reign of evil.

WHAT IS THE MYSTERY OF INIQUITY?

The word translated *iniquity* in the King James Version of the Bible, *anomia*, is better translated *lawlessness*. Paul was indeed writing about an era when the world, led by the Antichrist, will abandon the laws of God and embrace everything contrary to God's principles of righteousness. However, lawlessness is a by-product of iniquity, for "whoever commits sin also commits lawlessness, and *sin is lawlessness*" (1 John 3:4). The words, in this respect, can easily be used interchangeably.

What then is the *mystery of iniquity*? Considering our exploration of the word *musterion,* the *mystery* of iniquity would refer to the *secret* behind the manifestation of sin; that which empowers and enables the sons of men to commit transgression. This simplified explanation points to the spiritual phenomenon that instigates and promotes sin - the devil and his cohorts. Paul was referring to this concept when he wrote about "the prince of the power of the air, *the spirit who now **works** in the sons of disobedience*" (Ephesians 2:2). In other words, there is an active spirit, the prince of the power of the air, that is the root cause of lusts, evil desires, and opposition to God's laws. This spirit "now works." Although this does not absolve men and women of the consequences of their choice to walk in disobedience, the relevance of this mystery is evident.

THE MYSTERY OF GODLINESS VS THE MYSTERY OF LAWLESSNESS

Now, the above explanation of the mystery of iniquity, that there is a spirit at work wherever there is disobedience and sin, does not fully explain the impending manifestation of wide-spread lawlessness and the rise of the Antichrist. There should be a more substantive reason, one that justifies the need for the restraining ministry of the Holy Spirit. Understanding this dimension of the mystery of iniquity is, in fact, *the vital key* that has the immense potential to unlock our comprehension of end-time events and how the Antichrist will show up on the world's scene.

To gain deeper insight into the mystery of iniquity, let us consider what Paul said about a similar but opposite mystery - the mystery of *godliness*. I say "similar but opposite" because whilst the mystery of lawlessness relates to how the Antichrist's era of lawlessness will permeate the earth, the mystery of godliness relates to how God's kingdom of righteousness has already become a growing reality in the world. What

Paul said about the mystery of godliness is compelling.

> And without controversy **great is the mystery of godliness:** God was manifested in the flesh, Justified in the Spirit, Seen by angels, Preached among the Gentiles, Believed on in the world, Received up in glory.
>
> ### *(I Timothy 3:16)*

The great mystery behind the manifestation of godliness in the earth today started with the incarnation of God in the birth of Jesus and culminated in Christ's ascension to heaven after He paid the ultimate price for man's redemption. In-between these two powerful incidences are some spiritual realities, processes, and occurrences that sum up the mystery. At the apex of this six-fold mystery is the ascension of Christ, which was vital for the outpouring of the Holy Spirit and birth of the Church. The mystery of godliness is great indeed!

Likewise, we can view the mystery of lawlessness, not just as a simple reference to "the prince of the power of the air," but also as a few spiritual realities or incidences that are working together for the purpose of ushering in an era of lawlessness in the world spearheaded by the Antichrist.

Using the same approach that Paul adopted to describe the mystery of godliness, I have come up with a few mirror statements that could sum up the mystery of lawlessness.

- Lucifer became corrupted in heaven.

- Was seen by angels.

- Manifested in the garden of Eden.

- Was crushed by the Seed of the woman.

- Persecutes the remnant seed.

- Actively prepares for and awaits his time to completely dominate the world with law-lessness.

Let us briefly explore biblical evidence for each of these statements to gain a complete view of the mystery of lawlessness.

1. Lucifer became corrupted in heaven

Lucifer was one of the first angels God created. He was an archangel responsible for music and worship in heaven. He walked in the presence of God until a time when iniquity was found in him. Scholars agree that Ezekiel's lamentation for the king of Tyre is a direct reference to Lucifer's beginnings

> *Son of man, take up a lamentation for the king of Tyre, and say to him, 'Thus says the Lord God: "You were the seal of perfection, Full of wisdom and perfect in beauty. You were in Eden, the garden of God; Every precious stone was your*

*covering: The sardius, topaz, and diamond, Beryl, onyx, and jasper, Sapphire, turquoise, and emerald with gold. The workmanship of your timbrels and pipes Was prepared for you on the day you were created. "You were the anointed cherub who covers; I established you; You were on the holy mountain of God; You walked back and forth in the midst of fiery stones. You were perfect in your ways from the day you were created, **Till iniquity was found in you.**"*

(Ezekiel 28:12-15)

Another prophecy by Isaiah expounds on the *kind* of iniquity that formed in Lucifer's heart: he wanted to ascend unto God's throne and gain authority over all creation.

*How you are fallen from heaven, O Lucifer, son of the morning! How you are cut down to the ground, You who weakened the nations! For you have said in your heart: '**I will ascend into heaven, I will exalt my throne above the stars of God;** I will also sit on the mount of the congregation On the farthest sides of the north; I will ascend above the heights of the clouds, **I will be like the Most High.**' Yet you shall be brought down to Sheol, To the lowest depths of the Pit.*

(Isaiah 14:12-15)

The testimony of these two prophets affirms the truth about Lucifer's origins and intentions. He was created perfectly but got corrupted by the sin he brewed in his heart.

2. Lucifer was seen by angels

After Lucifer nurtured the desire to occupy God's throne, he managed to convince "a third of the stars of heaven," the angelic host, to join him in his rebellion against God (Revelation 12:4). They waged a war against the Most High but lost to Michael, God's warrior archangel, who resisted and defeated him.

> And war broke out in heaven: Michael and his angels fought with the dragon; and the dragon and his angels fought, but they did not prevail, nor was a place found for them in heaven any longer. **So the great dragon was cast out, that serpent of old, called the Devil and Satan,** who deceives the whole world; **he was cast to the earth, and his angels were cast out with him.**
>
> **(Revelation 12:7-9)**

All the angels of heaven, the third that sided with him and the two-thirds that remained loyal to God, were witnesses of Lucifer's ambition, rebellion, and expulsion. Till today, they are all active participants in the affairs the earth, either as a vast network of evil spirits, principalities, powers, rulers of the darkness of this age, and spiritual hosts of wickedness in the heavenly places (Ephesians 6:12), or as an even more vast host of "angels who excel in strength, who do God's word... and are "sent forth to minister for those who will inherit salvation" (Psalm 103:20 and Hebrews 1:14).

3. Lucifer manifested in the garden of Eden

God created Adam and Eve in His own image and gave them a mandate to administer the earth on His behalf. He authorised and mandated them to "be fruitful and multiply; fill the earth and subdue it; have dominion over the fish of the sea, over the birds of the air, and over every living thing that moves on the earth" (Genesis 1:26). He also gave them everything they needed for life and sustenance. Their mission was to begin from the garden of Eden.

However, Lucifer showed up in the garden, having possessed the body of a serpent, and lured the couple away from following God's simple law (see Genesis 3:1-8). Their act of disobedience led to them being separated from God and the relinquishing of their authority over the earth to the devil.

4. Lucifer's head was crushed by the Seed of the woman

Adam and Eve's disobedience caused sin and its consequence to rule over mankind. But God, in His foreknowledge, had already devised a plan to redeem man to Himself and reverse the curse of lawlessness that would enslave the generations of mankind. This plan was the great mystery of godliness mentioned above, the crux of which was the mission of Christ as the Seed of the woman who would crush the head of Lucifer.

> So the Lord God said to the serpent: "Because you have done this, you are cursed more than all cattle, and more than every beast of the field; on your belly you shall go, and you shall earth dust all the days of your life. And I will put enmity between you and the woman, and between your seed and her Seed; **He shall bruise your head, and you shall bruise His heel.**"
>
> **Genesis 3:14-15**

If the devil and "the rulers of this age" knew anything about this dimension of the mystery of godliness, "they would not have crucified the Lord of glory" (1 Corinthians 2:7-8). Hallelujah!

5. Lucifer persecutes the remnant seed

Ever since God declared that the serpent would bruise the heel of the seed of the woman, Satan had always gone after anyone who showed signs of being in covenant with God. From Abel to Joseph, from baby Moses to King David, from the prophets to the incarnate Christ, the devil has never ceased seeking to destroy the righteous seed. The best he has ever done, at least in his eyes at the time, was the persecution and crucifixion of Jesus Christ, which, we have noted, he would have done otherwise if he knew the wisdom of God.

Yet, even after his defeat, brought about by the cross of calvary, the devil is still gnawing at the heels of Christ, the heel being part of Christ's body, the Church. From Stephen, the first martyr of the church, to all who, throughout church history, have been put to death for their faith, even to the present day, the devil's evil antagonism is evident. He will continue to wage war against those "who keep the commandments of God and have the testimony of Jesus Christ" (Revelation 12:17).

6. Lucifer is actively preparing for and awaiting his time to completely dominate the world for a season

This has been the devil's primary aim since iniquity was found in him: to sit in God's seat, and gain dominion over the earth, the world's systems and all the people therein. In every generation, he and his evil spirits have actively recruited people, kings, and nobles, who would embrace and realise his ambition of a global, totalitarian era of lawlessness, one that opposes every law and precept of God. He lures men and women with the promise of wealth and power if only they can bow down to him, fuel his vision, and work tirelessly to bring it to fruition. He knows he has but a short time and will use every opportunity to accomplish his lofty goal.

IS THE STAGE NOW SET?

In the light of this overview of the mystery of lawlessness, one might ask the question, "Is the scene now set for the unveiling of the Anti-christ?" Are we any close to witnessing the rise of the man of sin? The Father alone knows the day or the hour, but there is a crucial and relevant insight about the mystery of lawlessness that we need to explore. Awareness of this operational dimension is a *vital key* in understanding the times and standing our ground against the devil's schemes. The moment you see this device for what it is, you will gain wisdom on how to navigate these perilous times.

5

HOW THE MYSTERY WORKS (1)

Paul made a revealing statement about the mystery of iniquity that is worthy of note. He said, "the mystery of lawlessness is *already* at work" (2 Thessalonians 2:7). In other words, the hidden agenda of the devil that facilitates and manifests as lawlessness was at work, even in Paul's day. It was not dormant or passive, but active and functional. This is a crucial point in understanding the signs of the time, for if the mystery of lawlessness was working when Paul wrote his epistle, and the purpose of the mystery to usher in the Antichrist is yet to be achieved, then we can expect the mystery to still be at work today.

So, what did Paul mean when he said, "the mystery of lawlessness is *already at work*"? How can we recognise the activity of this mystery today? We need to first go all the way back to the beginning and trace how this mystery has been working to facilitate lawlessness. Thereafter, we can observe these ancient traits in all that is happening in the world today.

THE MYSTERY AT WORK IN THE GARDEN

Employing the Bible study principle of noting where a concept is first mentioned or discussed in scripture, let us consider how the mystery of lawlessness worked in the garden of Eden. The devil approached Eve subtly in the form of a friendly serpent who seemed concerned about Eve's welfare. Concealing his identity and intention, he engaged Eve in conversation and sowed dubious thoughts about God into her mind. He then attacked God's law, questioned God's integrity, played down the consequence of disobedience, and painted a false picture of what Eve would gain if she acted against God's command. The mystery worked perfectly and achieved its purpose, which was to make Eve contravene God's express command. God had told Adam, and thus Eve, not to eat from the tree of the knowledge of good and evil, but "she took of its fruit and ate. She also gave it to her husband with her, and he ate" (see Genesis 3:1-8).

When God questioned Eve about her act of disobedience, the answer she gave was revealing. She said, "the serpent *deceived* me, and I ate" (Genesis 3:13). That was the mystery of lawlessness at work. The devil did not force Eve to disobey God, but he *deceived* her to such a point that she thought abandoning God's law was the right and beneficial thing to do.

> "So when the woman saw that the tree was **good for food**, that it was **pleasant to the eyes**, and a tree **desirable to make one wise**, she took of its fruit and ate."
>
> **(Genesis 3:6)**

The mystery of lawlessness was in full effect when Eve, the deceived, ate the fruit forbidden by God and "also gave to her husband with her, and he ate." Paul, in his letter to Timothy, said, "Adam was not deceived, but the woman *being deceived*, fell into transgression" (1 Timothy 2:13). Of course, Adam is not without blame because, although he knew better, he chose to *rebel* against God's law. Deception and rebellion are like turbo engines of the mystery of lawlessness that work in sync to accomplish the devil's purposes. They are both active processes that combine to produce lawlessness. This was evident in the story of man's fall from grace.

THE MYSTERY AT WORK IN HEAVEN

What about the story of Lucifer's fall from his lofty angelic position: can we trace these devices to the events that culminated in the expulsion of a third of the angelic order?

We have already seen from the prophecies of Isaiah and Ezekiel that the sin found in Lucifer's heart was his determined ambition to ascend God's throne. This ambition was fuelled by pride. His heart was lifted up because of his beauty, ability, and intrinsic value. A warped sense of self-importance and self-worth blinded him from the reality of God's almightiness. He forgot that he was created, and God was His Creator. This *self-deception* led to his rejection of God's authority and inevitable downfall.

"Pride," the Bible says, "goes before destruction, and a haughty spirit before a fall" (Proverbs 16:18). It makes the proud person focus on self to their own peril. This is why a church leader should not be "a novice, lest being puffed up with pride *he fall into the same condemnation as the devil*" (1 Timothy 3:7). Pride is a manifestation of self-deception.

> **The pride of your heart has deceived you,** You who dwell in the clefts of the rock, Whose habitation is high; You who say in your heart, 'Who will bring me down to the ground?'
>
> **(Obadiah 1:3)**
>
> **Your fierceness has deceived you, The pride of your heart**, O you who dwell in the clefts of the rock, Who hold the height of the

hill! Though you make your nest as high as the eagle, I will bring you down from there," says the Lord.

(Jeremiah 49:16)

Indeed, out of the mouth of two witnesses, this truth is affirmed: self-deception and rebellion were the dual characteristic of the mystery of lawlessness that led to Satan's expulsion from heaven. We do not know the exact words Lucifer spoke to a third of the angels, but they certainly would have been lies about God and false promises of promotion if he were the one on the throne. They became deceived as he was, joined in the rebellion against God's authority, and lost their place in heaven.

PHILOSOPHIES OF DECEPTION, SELF-DECEPTION, AND REBELLION

From these two instances of the mystery of lawlessness at work, there are certain things we can deduce, from God's perspective, about the concepts of deception, self-deception, and rebellion.

Philosophies of deception

- *The concealing of evil intentions is the bedrock of deception.* The devil will always hide his identity and plan from people he wants to deceive. He "transforms himself into an angel of light" to deceive those in the light (2 Corinthians 11:14).

- *Half-truths are equally dangerous as untruths.* A "little" lie mixed with truth will lead to a misinterpretation and misapplication of God's law. The devil is a master at twisting God's words for his own destructive ends.

- *An outright lie is a direct affront against truth.* When the serpent told Eve, "You shall *not surely die,*" not only was he lying; he was also calling God a liar.

- *The secret aim of a deceiver is to entrap victims and steal their freedoms.* The moment Adam and Eve disobeyed God's voice; they lost the freedom they once enjoyed in God's presence.

- *The danger of deception is its ability to lead the deceived to reject the standards and authority of God.* When deception runs its course, man will outrightly reject God's leadership and His laws.

- *When the devil speaks a lie, he is speaking his native language.* Jesus made this statement about the devil during one of His discourses (John 8:44), a statement of fact about the origin of lies.

- *Deception uses all the gates that lead to the mind and floods them with misinformation, lies, and enticement.* Before Eve took decisive action to disobey God, she "*saw* that the tree was good for food, that it was pleasant to the *eyes*, and a tree desirable to make one wise" (Genesis 3:6). The mystery of iniquity worked upon her as "the lust of the flesh, the lust of the eyes, and the pride of life" (1 John 2:16).

- *Where God and His laws are concerned, the deceiver and the deceived are both guilty of lawlessness.* Everyone is responsible for their actions before God. "I was deceived" is not a permissible excuse for lawlessness, especially if one had prior knowledge of the truth. Eve blamed the serpent; Adam blamed Eve; the serpent had no one to blame. They were all found guilty before God.

- *Deception is the birthplace of rebellion against God's righteous standards.* Wherever deception runs deep, lawlessness and rebellion against God become the order of the day.

Philosophies of self-deception

- *Pride and arrogance are breeding grounds for self-deception.* Paul, writing to the Galatians, said, "If anyone thinks himself to be something, when he is nothing, he *deceives* himself" (Galatians 6:3).

- *Self-deception blinds a person from clear logic and reason.* How can a created being question the authority of his creator? How can clay seek the same esteem as the Potter that fashions the clay (Isaiah 29:16)? Lucifer's prideful and disillusioned heart strayed into realms of irrationality.

- *The estimation a self-deceived person has of him or herself usually contradicts reality.* Ezekiel gave this prophecy against the prince of Tyre: "Because your heart is lifted up, And you say, 'I am a god, I sit in the seat of gods, In the midst of the seas,' *Yet you are a man, and not a god*, Though you set your heart as the heart of a god" (Ezekiel 28:2). Jesus also said the following about the church in Laodicea: "You say, 'I am rich, have become wealthy, and have need of nothing' —*and do not know that you are wretched, miserable, poor, blind, and naked*" (Revelation 3:17).

- *Self-deception leads to a direct confrontation with the authority and laws of God.* The more Lucifer nurtured his ideas fuelled by self-deception, the closer he came to outrightly rejecting God's authority. War was the outcome that restored order in heaven.

- *Self-deception inevitably leads to lawlessness and rebellion.* Again, self-deception, lawlessness, and rebellion have similar roots. Self-deception starts as a seed in the heart. Its first fruit is lawlessness, and the harvest is rebellion.

- *In his mind, a self-deceived person thinks he is right and everyone else is wrong.* When a person believes his own lies, he will usually lose every sense of objectivity to engage with opinions that are different to his.

- *Self-deception makes a person a law unto himself.* A self-deceived person only believes himself and those who are similarly deceived. He rewrites the law book of life and rejects the divine laws of God. This is the root of lawlessness.

- *A self-deceived person will always look for those who will agree with his or her point of view.* In order to fortify his position, a self-deceived person will always gravitate towards those who share the same opinion.

- *Let him who thinks he stands take heed lest he falls.* The consequence of uncorrected self-deception is always a fall. If the deceptive seed is growing within, a fall will follow in time. Appearing to stand when deception has taken root in the heart can only fool people. But the true state of the heart will become evident when the deceived falls.

Philosophies of rebellion against God

- *Rebellion against God occurs when man knowingly rejects God's law in favour of perceived pleasure or self-interest.* The serpent succeeded in making Eve think that God was standing in the way of her pleasure and enjoyment. Adam thought the same and rebelled against God's authority.

- *Rebellion against God is the act of severing one's allegiance to God and pledging allegiance to the devil.* This was the case with the third of angels. It was also the case with the first couple, even if they did not know this would be the consequence of their actions.

- *Rebellion against God is the conscious disregard of the overwhelming body of evidence about the goodness and providence of God.* Adam and Eve had no excuse to sin because God gave them all things to enjoy. Today, some cite the injustice, inequality, and suffering in the world as excuses to rebel against God, but they choose to ignore the weight of evidence in nature about God's power, love, and goodness.

- *Rebellion against God is like the sin of witchcraft.* Prophet Samuel made this statement to King Saul when he disobeyed God (1 Samuel 15:23). A person may seek to do

God's will but not in God's way. This is also rebellion. The flesh cannot accomplish God's will and there is no amount of manipulation that would get Him to endorse wrongdoing.

- *The one who rebels against God cannot say "the devil made me rebel."* Adam blamed Eve, and Eve blamed the serpent; but each one received the just reward of their rebellion.

- *Rebellion against God robs one of a relationship and privileges with God.* Adam and Eve lost their access to God and their place in the garden. They lost their authority over the earth and became slaves to the devil.

- *Rebellion against God is the ultimate goal of lawlessness.* The devil had already rejected God's authority, and through deception leading to rebellion, he led Adam and Eve on this same path of destruction.

Evidently, these philosophies of deception, self-deception, and rebellion are key to understanding the dynamics of the mystery of iniquity, the impact it has had from the beginning of time, and how we can recognise its traits today.

THE MYSTERY AT WORK IN PAUL'S DAY

When Paul said, "the mystery of lawlessness is *already* at work," he was aware of the deceptive activities of the evil one in his day. This was one of the reasons why he wrote his epistles to the churches, to confront and halt the flow of deception in the church. Early on in his letter to the Thessalonians, he had said, "Let no one *deceive* you by any means" (2 Thessalonians 2:3). Wherever he preached and raised disciples, he was always particular about protecting the saints from deception and heresies and equipping them to do likewise.

After three years of ministry in Ephesus, on the day he was going to entrust the saints into the hands of other shepherds, Paul said the following heartfelt words:

> Take care and be on guard for yourselves and for the whole flock over which the Holy Spirit has appointed you as overseers, to shepherd (tend, feed, guide) the church of God which He bought with His own blood. I know that after I am gone, [false teachers like] ferocious wolves will come in among you, not sparing the flock; even from among your own selves men will arise, **speaking perverse and distorted things, to draw away the disciples after themselves** [as their followers]. Therefore be continually alert, remembering that for three years, night or day, I did not stop admonishing and advising each one [of you] with tears.
>
> **(Acts 20:28-31 AMP)**

Paul and all the early church fathers constantly had to deal with "false apostles, deceitful workers," and false teachers, who paraded themselves as and transformed "themselves into apostles of Christ" (2 Corinthians 11:13). Paul said the messages of such people "spread like cancer... and they overthrow the faith of some" (2 Timothy 2:17-18). Even Jesus warned against religious teachers and erroneous teachings that work like harmful leaven, corrupting the minds of those that embrace them (Matthew 15:5-12). The first thing He said when asked about the signs of the end of time was, "take heed that no one deceives you" (Matthew 24:4).

The way the devil beguiled Adam and Eve in the garden, twisting God's words with an aim to turn the couple away from following God's law, is the same way he has consistently sought to distort truth in the church. This mystery of lawlessness has, throughout church history, manifested in the form of various heresies and false teachings.

For example, Paul named "Hymenaeus and Philetus... who have strayed concerning the truth, saying the resurrection is already past" (2 Timothy 2:17). This was an erroneous teaching like the one that claimed Christ had already come. Some of these teachings bluntly denied some foundational doctrines of the faith, including the incarnation or deity of Christ. Others just twist the scriptures "to their own destruction" (2 Peter 3:16).

In its original usage, the Greek word *hairesis* simply meant a body of philosophical thoughts and opinions around a particular subject. It was a neutral term. However, when "thoughts and opinions" about some fundamental truths relating to Christ and His mission to redeem mankind were evidently off the mark, it was important that church leaders rose to truth's defence. For instance, a portion of Paul's first letter to the Corinthians was written to expound the doctrine and mystery of resurrection because some were communicating the *hairesis* "that there is no resurrection of the dead" (1 Corinthians 15:12). Or consider doctrines that encourage a believer to sin freely because Christ had paid the ultimate price for our redemption once and for all. On this, John the apostle wrote, "*Let no one deceive you.* He who practices righteousness is righteous, just as He is righteous. He who sins is of the devil, for the devil has sinned from the beginning" (1 John 3:7-8).

It cannot be overstated that Apostolic leaders in the church have a responsibility to equip the saints with truth that can withstand error. This is necessary so that believers are no longer "tossed to and fro and carried about with every wind of doctrine by the *trickery of men, in the cunning craftiness of deceitful plotting*" (Ephesians 4:14).

Some doctrinal errors attack the fundamental tenets of faith, godliness, and the cornerstone of our relationship with God. They misinterpret and misapply the teachings of Christ. Others completely deny the authenticity of the person of Christ and disapprove of His deity. For example, *Docetism* was a body of heretical teachings that asserted that Christ did not come in the flesh because they reckon all flesh and matter to be impure. Christ, according to this heresy, was only spirit, contradicting orthodox understanding of Christ being fully God and fully man. Docetism denied the virgin birth of Christ, and claimed that His crucifixion, resurrection, and ascension were only apparitions. Docetic ideologies and doctrines were major assaults on the truth about Christ. They opposed Christ, His redemptive work, and His church.

OPPOSING CHRIST

Evidently, the mystery of iniquity, manifesting as deception, lies, and heresies, was active in Paul's day and throughout church history. It is still active today. Through the activity of different entities, the mystery opposed Christ, His church and everything Christ stood for. The word *antichrist* is made up of two words, *anti,* which means "against" or "opposed to," and *Christ* or *Christos*, and there is a clear link between the mystery of iniquity and that which stands in opposition to the person and authority of Christ. John, the apostle, established this association in his epistles.

> *Little children, it is the last hour; and as you have heard that **the Antichrist is coming**, even now **many antichrists have come**, by which we know that it is the last hour... Who is a liar but he who denies that Jesus is the Christ? **He is antichrist** who denies the Father and the Son. Whoever denies the Son does not have the Father either; he who acknowledges the Son has the Father also... These things I have written to you concerning those who try to deceive you.*

(1 John 2:18,22-23,26)

John made a distinction between "the Antichrist" who was to come, and the "many antichrists" that were already in existence. The yet-to-come Antichrist is the man of sin Paul referred to in his letter to the Thessalonians (we will discover more about him in chapter 8), and the "many antichrists" were various entities that opposed Christ and His truth, the mystery of iniquity working tirelessly to oppose godliness and establish lawlessness in the earth. These entities are people and the spirits working through them behind the scenes. John called this association "the spirit of the Antichrist," the deceptive operation that has one aim - to suppress truth and usher in an era of lawlessness.

> *Beloved, do not believe every spirit, but test the spirits, whether they are of God; because many false prophets have gone out into the world. By this you know the Spirit of God: Every spirit that confesses that Jesus Christ has come in the flesh is of God, and every spirit that does not confess that Jesus Christ has come in the flesh is not of God.* **And this is the spirit of the Antichrist**, *which you have heard was coming, and is now already in the world.*
>
> **(1 John 4:1-3)**

The "spirit of the Antichrist" is the mystery of lawlessness in manifestation, the mystery that is already working. "For many *deceivers* have gone out into the world who do not confess Jesus Christ as coming in the flesh. *This is a deceiver and an antichrist*" (2 John 1:7).

OPPOSING TRUTH

Jesus said, "I am the way, *the truth,* and the life" (John 14:6). However, the spirit of the Antichrist and the entities that work with it are vehemently and fundamentally opposed to these claims. They will do anything possible to divert people from the way, curtail the spread of truth, and squash expressions of God's life. Let us consider three instances of this antichrist agenda.

Anti-resurrection propaganda

When "the rulers of this age" conspired to crucify Jesus, the Lord of glory, they thought that would mark His end. But on the third day, just as He predicted, Christ rose from the grave and appeared to some of the women who had visited the place where He was buried. With great joy, they went to share the good news with the rest of the disciples.

When the religious leaders who had played a part in Christ's crucifixion learnt about what had happened, they conspired to propagate a lie to counter the news of Christ's resurrection.

> *Now while they were going, behold, some of the guard came into the city and reported to the chief priests all the things that had happened. When they had assembled with the elders and consulted together,* ***they gave a large sum of money to the soldiers, saying, "Tell them, 'His disciples came at night and stole Him away while we slept.'*** *And if this comes to the governor's ears, we will appease him and make you secure." So they took the money and did as they were instructed; and* ***this saying is commonly reported among the Jews until this day.***
>
> **(Matthew 28:11-15)**

This is a classic case of how those who oppose truth seek to sway people away from the knowledge of Christ. They invested heavily into a false narrative about Christ's empty tomb, claiming that the disciples stole His body at night. As absurd as this may sound, the lie is still spreading today. There are other fabrications like this that propagate speculative theories about the person of Christ, including claims that He sojourned in India and had a romantic relationship with Mary Magdalene. The sole purpose of these lies is to divert people from the way of faith, truth, and salvation.

Anti-gospel cancel culture

Lies cannot easily overcome the person who has had an encounter with truth. The risen Christ, at various times, appeared to His disciples, to "five hundred brethren at once," and to those who would later congregate in the Upper Room prior to the day of Pentecost. Not only did He show Himself to His disciples; He also gave them infallible proofs about His resurrection, ate with them, and spoke extensively about the Kingdom. He commissioned them to take the good news of the Kingdom to the ends of the earth; He ascended into heaven before their eyes and promised to return later.

The authenticity of these encounters with Christ, as well as the enduement of power that the believers experienced on the day of Pentecost, meant that the propagation of sponsored lies about Christ's body could not withstand the impact of truth. Many people believed the message of the apostles and signs, wonders, and miracles were occurring daily.

So, in order to counter the powerful advance of the church, the religious rulers challenged the apostles on the authority with which they preached and did miracles. They commanded them "not to speak at all nor teach in the name of Jesus" (Acts 4:18). When a simple command failed to have the required effect, they "laid their hands on the apostles and put them in the common prison." They even flogged them and forbid them to speak in the name of Jesus. Rather than stop talking about Jesus, the apostles rejoiced "that they were counted worthy to suffer shame for His name... they did not cease teaching and preaching Jesus as the Christ (Acts 5:40-42). Every attempt to intimidate the apostles and cancel their message failed woefully.

Anti-truth death crusade

The enemy of truth, realising that the lies and threats were not doing much to slow down the advance of the church, he took his attacks to a new level. Focusing his attention on Stephen, a deacon of the church who was "full of faith and power," he moved the religious leaders to "secretly [induce] men" to lie against Stephen.

"They stirred up the people, the elders, and the scribes" against him, and "set up false witnesses" to testify falsely against him. Despite all the powerful evidence that Stephen shared about the validity of his message about the Lordship of Christ, the people "stopped their ears," dragged him to the edge of the city, and stoned him to death (see Acts 7:54-60).

This was the beginning of severe persecution of those who held unto the truths of the gospel, one that persisted throughout church history and is still prevalent today.

Ironically, the man, Saul, who was at the forefront of this initial wave of persecution, ended up committing his life to Christ after encountering Jesus on the road to Damascus. He later became Paul, the apostle. He knew first-hand how the mystery of lawlessness operated through secret councils and restrictive legislations, all aimed at curtailing and crushing truth. However, the more the disciples were put to the sword, the more the gospel spread. Surely, the gates of hell cannot prevail against the church.

6

HOW THE MYSTERY WORKS (2)

From the moment iniquity formed in his heart and he led an angelic rebellion against God, the goal of Lucifer was to exercise authority over all creation from the throne of God. Through lies and deception, he got the first Adam to disobey God and gained authority over the earth, which was originally bestowed upon man. God then spoke about the mystery of godliness, His redemption plan to restore man to Himself. This plan would see Christ, the Seed of the woman, crush the head of the devil and restore man's relationship with God. The devil, on the other hand, will bruise the heel of Christ.

Let us consider this prophecy again.

> *And I will put enmity (open hostility) between you and the woman, and between your seed (offspring) and her Seed; He shall [fatally]*

bruise your head, and you shall [only] bruise His heel.

(Genesis 3:15 AMP)

It is safe to say most scholars believe that, amongst other things, this declaration relates to events of the Cross, where Christ, through His death and resurrection, conquered death, sin, and the works of Satan. He dealt a fatal death blow on the devil and set man free from the power of sin forever. Indeed, God, through Christ, *"has delivered us from the power of darkness* and conveyed us into the kingdom of the Son of His love, in whom we have redemption through His blood, the forgiveness of sins" (Colossians 1:13-14). Yes, He *"disarmed the rulers and authorities* [those supernatural forces of evil operating against us], He made a public example of them [exhibiting them as captives in His triumphal procession], having triumphed over them through the cross" (Colossians 2:15 AMP).

Surely, the enmity between the seed of lawlessness and the Seed of godliness, to use those terms, raged on after man was driven out of the garden of Eden, with Cain killing Abel being a classic manifestation of this conflict. However, this Eden prophecy focused on the culmination of this hostility - the complete victory of Christ, the Seed of the woman, over the devil. Notice that, according to the prophecy, the bruising of the serpent's head would come first: "He will bruise your head, and you shall bruise His heel." If the resurrection of Christ crushed Satan's head, an action that precedes the bruising of the heel, what does the latter refer to?

Many scholars refer to the sufferings of Christ and eventual death on the cross as the bruising of the heel - a temporary wound with no fatal consequences. This may be the case considering the conjunction "and" in the Eden prophecy ("He will bruise your head, *and* you shall bruise His heel," which suggests concurrent actions).

However, the prophecy *starts* with the crushing of the devil's head, not the bruising of Christ's heel (which may also suggest sequential actions). Besides, the passion of Christ and the sufferings He endured leading to the crucifixion were not inflicted on Him *by* the devil. Satan thought he was the one afflicting Christ, but he did not know what he was doing. If he did, he "would not have crucified the Lord of glory" (1 Corinthians 2:8).

The sufferings and death that Jesus endured were direct actions of God, the Father, as He sought to redeem man through this eternal sacrifice. The prophecy of Isaiah about the suffering Messiah states clearly that He, Christ, "has borne our griefs and carried our sorrows; yet we esteemed Him stricken, *smitten by God, and afflicted*. But He was wounded *for* our transgressions, He was bruised *for* our iniquities; the chastisement *for* our peace was upon Him, and by His stripes we are healed... He had done no violence, nor was any deceit in His mouth. *Yet it pleased the Lord to bruise Him*" (Isaiah 53:4-5,9-10). It was God the Father who bruised the Seed of the woman, His Son, the Christ, not the devil! He bruised Him *for* our transgressions, iniquities, and peace. The devil would not bruise Him for any of these. Just as Abraham declared on the mountain of Moriah, God provided "*for Himself* the lamb for a burnt offering" (Genesis 22:8).

When Peter tried to defend Jesus with a sword, Jesus said to him, "Put your sword into the sheath. Shall I not drink the cup which *My Father* has given Me?" (John 18:11). And to Pilate who thought he had the power to crucify or release Jesus, He said "You could have no power at all against Me unless it had been given you from above" (John 19:11). The devil had no power over Christ. All he could do was nibble at the heel of Christ *after* the Lord had risen from the dead and birthed the Church, which is His body. He has been striking the heel of the Church ever since, but the God of peace has a plan to shortly crush Satan *under* the feet of the Church (Romans 16:20).

THE MYSTERY IN PROPER PERSPECTIVE

Thus, it is important we understand the mystery of iniquity from God's perspective and see that God is never taken unawares no matter what the devil does. Without this understanding, we would only see the evil that Satan is doing in the world and think we are at his mercy. This is far from the truth. Yes, the mystery of iniquity is very much at work, but God is not intimidated by the enemy's schemes. As "the kings of the earth set themselves, and the rulers take counsel together, against the Lord and against his anointed," working in and manifesting the spirit of the antichrist, *"He who sits in the heavens shall laugh; the Lord shall hold them in derision"* (Psalm 2:2-4). Christ laid down His life for mankind. He is building His church on the earth, and the gates of hell cannot prevail over this pillar of truth.

This was the mindset of the apostles when the religious council threatened and persecuted them. Inspired by the above messianic psalm (Psalm 2), they prayed unto God and resolved to continue speaking the word with boldness. "And with great power the apostles gave witness to the resurrection of the Lord Jesus. And great grace was upon them all" (see Acts 4:23-33). We need the same kind of mindset, boldness, and commitment to mission no matter what the enemy throws at us.

ATTACKS FROM WITHIN

From the early days of the church, the mystery of iniquity worked intensely to stop the church from growing. The more it tried, through persecution, propaganda, and threats of death, the more "the word of the Lord grew and prevailed" (Acts 19:20; 12:24). As we noted in the previous chapter, there were many false teachings and teachers that bombarded the church. These were attacks from within the church, seeking to derail the truth of the gospel.

> *"Little children, it is the last hour; and as you have heard that the Antichrist is coming, even now many antichrists have come, by which we know that it is the last hour.* **They went out from us, but they were not of us; for if they had been of us, they would have continued with us; but they went out that they might be made manifest, that none of them were of us.***"*
>
> *(1 John 2:18-19)*

The early church fathers battled earnestly to preserve the faith that was delivered to the church. Through a series of church councils, apostolic leaders met to agree on what constitutes the fundamental doctrines of the faith. For example, the council of Nicaea (AD 325) and the subsequent council held in Constantinople (AD 381) produced what is known as the Nicene

Creed, a set of doctrinal statements accepted widely as representative of the truths entrusted to the Church (see Appendix 1).

All these measures by the early church fathers, even in the face of widespread persecution, sought to mitigate against the mystery of iniquity operating within the church. Even with that, the church did not always get things right. To this day and until the Lord returns, there is a need to take a stand against doctrinal errors that seek to lead people away from the truth.

ATTACKS FROM WITHOUT

After more than two millennia of the Church's existence, we can confidently say that the gates of hell have not prevailed over her. They have tried all sorts to contain, dilute, and destroy her testimony, but God's people have continued to multiply and wax strong. God is aware that "while men slept, his enemy came and sowed tares among the wheat" of the church, yet He is not perturbed. He is committed to the body of Christ in the earth and will continue to "*sanctify and cleanse her with the washing of water by the word,* that He might present her to Himself a glorious church, not having spot or wrinkle or any such thing, but that she should be holy and without blemish" (Ephesians 5:26-27).

The devil has not relented in his efforts to subdue the Church. Not only has he continued to attack the Church from within, the greater and perhaps more viscous manifestations of the mystery of iniquity have been from outside the church. This outworking of evil is not only attempting to *rival* and *infiltrate* the Church; it is also actively preparing the grounds for the rise of the man of sin, the Antichrist. The grand aim of the devil and those who buy into his vision is to subdue the whole world under a regime of lawlessness, and the mystery of iniquity is still working to accomplish this today. The primary tools are still lies, deception, and all the vices that facilitate rebellion against God.

Almost everywhere we turn, the mystery of iniquity is evident and active. This is not magnifying the devil or denying God's ownership of "the world and those who dwell therein," rather it is an acknowledgement of the truth of God's word that a time has been appointed for the evil one to assume total authority over the earth, howbeit for short a season, until he meets his destruction.

> *"We know that we are of God, and the whole world lies under the sway of the wicked one."*
>
> ***(1 John 5:19)***

Let us briefly consider some of the facets or manifestations of the mystery of lawlessness in the world today that is not only keeping people under the devil's sway, preventing them to see the light of the gospel of Christ, but also preparing a conducive environment for the Antichrist to emerge and fulfil end-time prophecy.

SECRET SOCIETIES

Ironically, for the first three centuries after Pentecost, the church endured severe persecution because of the "haireses" (opinions and philosophies) about Christ that she taught and promoted. The message of the cross of Christ was setting people free from the power of sin and death, yet the world branded it offensive. Due to severe persecution in the early years by the religious class as well as different Roman emperors, the church operated "in secret," more like the "underground church" today.

However, a new era emerged when emperor Constantine, who had affinity for the Christian community, partly because his mother was Christian, made Christianity the official state religion of Rome. He was the one who called for the council of Nicaea in AD 325 to harmonise and standardise the various factions of the Christian message. As noted previously, this council, and its predecessor council, adopted the Nicene Creed as the foundational doctrinal positions of the Church. Any teaching that conflicted with these cardinal truths were officially labelled heretical. The tide had changed dramatically.

As the influence of the institutionalised church grew[1], those with opposing ideologies receded into the shadows of mediaeval existence, and out of the shadows began to emerge the phenomena known as "secret societies."

By definition, a *secret society* is a group or organisation whose members bond together around a common purpose, ideology, belief, or practice, and usually swear an oath to conceal the group's activities. Membership is restricted to those who embrace the group's ground-level ethos, and undergo initiation rituals, which usually include vows of secrecy. Often, there are multiple membership levels within the group's hierarchy, and the higher a person goes, the more initiation rites he must undergo and "secrets" he must keep.

On the surface, some secret societies seem "harmless," while the objectives and practices of others are, from the church's perspective, opposed to the mystery of godliness, for example, freemasonry, Rosicrucianism, and the illuminati, to name a few.

In the following sections, we will discuss, howbeit, briefly some of these phenomena, most of which are still playing out in today's world.

Freemasonry

Arguably the largest secret society in the world that began around the 13th to 14th century, freemasonry consists of an association of people who fraternise around a common brotherhood and are known for a variety of rites, symbolisms, rituals, progressive ranks, ceremonies, and initiation ceremonies. Membership is conditioned on the belief in a supreme being and initiation vows are made on a religious book, which could be the Bible or any other sacred text. Meetings, initiation ceremonies, and social events are held within lodges in different jurisdictions around the world.

Rosicrucianism

This is another example of a spiritual order that began in the 17th century and claimed to offer people access to mystical knowledge about the world, the universe, and the spiritual realm. The blend of Christian mysticism, ancient philosophy, metaphysics, and occultism that the Rosicrucian order offered, attracted many esoteric people, who delight in supposedly exclusive or hidden knowledge.

The Illuminati

The original secret society called the Bavarian Illuminati started in Bavaria, Germany, in the year 1776, with stated goals to oppose superstitious beliefs, religious influence on public life, and the abuses of authority exerted by the monarchy.[2] They sought to gain control over society by infiltrating places of influence, including religious groups, freemasonry, and the royal quarters. Like most secret societies, they also had their secret codes, symbols, hierarchical degrees, and rites. Within ten years, they managed to attract many people of high standing, including intellectuals, politicians, royals, and businessmen. However, the government of Bavaria clamped down on the secret society, exposed their activities, published some of their artefacts, and imprisoned some of the members.

Although the original Order of the Illuminati no longer exists, it is widely believed that the ideologies and intent that formed the society survived by going underground. Some claim that the Illuminati was responsible for the 1789-1799 *French Revolution*, which radically changed the societal order in France and surrounding regions from church-and-monarchy-dominated societies to constitution-and-state-governed societies. Some publications and media production continue to fuel the notion that the Illuminati or their vision to control the world is alive and well today.

New World Order

The "New World Order" (NWO) is a term used to describe a supposed secret, sinister agenda that some powerful elites nurture to form a single world government that would rule over all nations and control the affairs of all people. Those who seek to unravel this so-called secretive agenda are usually branded "conspiracy theorists," meaning they are peddlers of untruths, half-truths, or unverifiable fabrications. Some of the theorists, including Christian eschatologists, have referenced the modern-day Illuminati and freemasons movement as part of the brain behind the NWO.

The NWO "conspiracy theory" remains at large as the world becomes increasingly globalised, and issues of cross-national concern are being addressed from a one-world perspective (for instance, viral disease control, money laundering, and climate change). Could it be that the issue is labelled a "conspiracy theory" just to deflect those who desire the truth of the matter? In recent times, some so-called "conspiracy theories" have turned out to be factual. Besides, deliberations about a single governance approach to world problems are no longer done in secret. The gathering of elites at the World Economic Forum (WEF) to discuss the *Global Reset* agenda is considered by some a point in question.

Satanism

As a collective description, "satanism" relates to a set of philosophies and practices promoted by groups that base their beliefs on "Satan," be it Satan as a deity (theistic satanism) or an ideological concept (atheistic satanism). Groups that identify with Satan have historically operated as secret societies. However, since the turn of the twentieth century, many are now recognised as public entities, particularly atheistic satanism or non-religious satanism. Such groups include the Church of Satan, Satanic Church, and Satanic Temple, many of which promote unrestrained carnality, immorality, and sensuality.

Luciferianism and other forms of devil worship are branches of satanism. The devil will give anything for people to bow down to him, just as he offered Jesus the world in exchange for a moment of worship (Matthew 4:8-9). Those who practice religious satanism and devil worship usually engage in various forms of rituals, blood sacrifices, magic, occultism, and orgies.

Secularism and Humanism

From the 17th and 18th centuries, during what was known as the age of enlightenment, many European countries began to shift away from the idea of religious beliefs being the basis for societal engagement. They sought to reduce the role and influence of the church over civic life by elevating reason, material considerations, and natural explanations over spiritual or superstitious standpoints. This philosophical development was, in part, also the basis for the separation of religion from the affairs of the state. Many countries have now embraced a wide spectrum of secularism, ranging from a total clamping down on religion to a tolerance of all religions alongside a secular society.

Humanism, which considers human beings as the sole determiner of morality, existence, and social experience, outrightly rejects religion or any form of religious interference in communal life. This philosophical stance has worked well within the secularism movement to advocate for increasingly less references to any form of divine authority in public, for example the outlawing of prayer in government schools. According to secular and humanistic ideologies, God is no longer the gold standard for truth; rather, truth is relative and subject to individual preferences, perspectives, and priorities.

THE SIMPLICITY OF THE GOSPEL

As Paul wrote, *"The mystery of lawlessness is already at work."* The sections above are just snippets of the enormous number of agencies, both past and present, working together to keep mankind from encountering and embracing the truths of God. They show that, even today, the wicked one continues to blind the minds of those who do not believe, lest the light of the gospel of the glory of Christ should shine on them (2 Corinthians 4:4). He keeps people away from the truth by occupying their minds with deceptive and destructive ideologies, activities, and associations.

Yet, there is power in the simplicity of the gospel message! All the conflict within the church and the moral attacks from outside have not hindered those who call on the Lord's name from getting saved! God continues to make foolish the wisdom of this world! Anyone who believes in Jesus Christ, the One who died and rose again from the grave, will cross from death unto life! They will escape the corruption that is in the world through lust! They will obtain a living hope of eternity with God!

If after trying everything you are still weighed down by the burden of sin; if deep down in your heart you know that you have not found the peace of God that passes all understanding. If all the philosophical arguments that oppose God have not eased your fears and uncertainties about what will happen to you after death; then you need to believe in the simplicity of the gospel of Christ.

If you confess with your mouth the Lord Jesus **and believe in your heart** that God has raised Him from the dead, **you will be saved.** For with the heart one believes unto righteousness, and with the mouth confession is made unto salvation.

(Romans 10:9-10)

Pray this simple prayer to invite Jesus into your life and heart.

Dear God,

I acknowledge my sinful state and my desperate need for a Saviour. I believe in my heart that Jesus died for me on the cross and conquered death when He rose from the grave. I confess Jesus as my Lord and Saviour and receive Him into my heart. I dedicate the rest of my life to worshipping you, living for you, and telling others about you. Amen.

7

THE INCREASE OF INIQUITY
& THE FALLING AWAY

In his letter to the Thessalonians, Paul made an emphatic statement about the coming of Christ:

> Let no one deceive you by any means; for that Day will not come **unless the falling away comes first**, and the man of sin is revealed, the son of perdition,
>
> ### (2 Thessalonians 2:3)

We have already illustrated this statement as a prophetic timeline of events that will lead to Christ's coming and the resurrection of the saints

The falling away	**The return of Christ**

Fig. 1

The revealing of the man of sin

Our gathering to Him

We have also explored what can be described as the main facilitator or enabler of the Antichrist's rise to prominence, the "man of sin" as Paul stated, which is the mystery of iniquity (lawlessness). The crucial instruments in the out-working of this mystery are lies and deception, which lead to iniquity, and culminate in rebellion. All these, according to God's word, are working together to usher in an era of lawlessness with the Antichrist as its primary spearhead.

We will, in the next chapter, examine the nature and mission of the Antichrist. However, in keeping with the exposition of Paul's epistle, what did he mean by "the falling away"? How does this relate to the things we have discovered thus far? These themes will be the focus of this chapter.

THE INCREASE OF INIQUITY

Jesus, in His discussion about end-time events, made a telling statement that can help us understand this "falling away" prediction.

> *Then many false prophets will rise up and deceive many. And **because lawlessness will abound**, the love of many will grow cold.*
>
> **(Matthew 24:11-12)**

Straightaway, we notice the mystery of iniquity operating as deception through false prophets. We then see that there will be an abundance of lawlessness, which would be the reason why the love of many people will grow cold. This abundance of lawlessness (which, by the way, is the goal of the Antichrist) will happen incrementally; it will not happen suddenly. Other Bible versions make this clear:

> Because **lawlessness is increased**, the love of most people will grow cold.
>
> **(Matthew 24:12 AMP)**

> Because of **the increase of wickedness**, the love of most will grow cold.
>
> **(Matthew 24:12 NIV)**

So, in the last days, there will be an unmistakable increase in the *manifestation* of iniquity and wickedness, which presupposes an increase in the *mystery* of iniquity and deception. If deception facilitates iniquity, then an increase in deception will lead to an increase in iniquity.

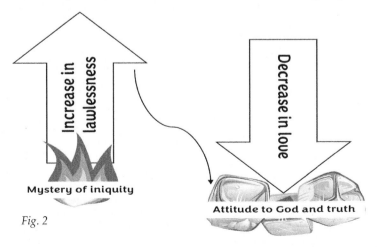

Fig. 2

We have already noted how this mystery has played out in the pervasive activities of false teachers, secret societies, humanistic ideologies, and secular movements. The following scripture, however, makes an explicit connection between increased iniquity and deception.

> But *evil men and impostors will grow worse and worse,* **deceiving and being deceived**.
>
> ### *(2 Timothy 3:13)*

In other words, the worsening of man's moral condition in the last days would be attributable to the increased activities of "evil men and impostors," evidenced by an increase in self-deception and intentional acts of deceit; and the increase in self-deception and deceit will in turn worsen man's moral condition. This is an ever-widening loop of lawlessness that only the restraining presence and activities of the Holy Spirit can curtail. Surely, "when the enemy comes in like a flood, the Spirit of the Lord will lift up a standard against him" (Isaiah 59:19). When, however, the Holy Spirit relaxes His ministry of restraining evil, the whole earth will be covered with a deluge of lawlessness and rebellion.

Notice also from this scripture that Paul mentions "evil men" and "impostors." An *impostor*, according to Dictionary.com, is "a person who *practices deception* under an assumed character, identity or name." The Oxford Learner's

Dictionary defines an impostor as "a person who *pretends* to be somebody else *in order to trick people.*" Furthermore, Oxford Languages states that an impostor is "a person who *pretends* to be someone else *in order to deceive others, especially for fraudulent gain.*" The Greek word used in this verse, *goace*, means "a wizard, sorcerer, enchanter, juggler, cheat, impostor." Therefore, associated closely to the increase of iniquity in the last days is the dubious activities of evil, deceptive, fraudulent, and cunning men parading themselves in the church as messengers of the gospel, and these would be directly or indirectly responsible for the love of many waxing cold.

WIZARDS, MAGICIANS, AND FRAUDSTERS

This point needs to be stressed. When Paul and Barnabas sought to share the good news with the proconsul at the island of Paphos, he was withstood by "Elymas the sorcerer," who was also a false prophet. Paul, under the anointing of the Spirit, confronted him sternly. The way Paul addressed him gives us useful insight into this issue of impostors in the church.

> **"O full of all deceit and all fraud**, you son of the devil, you enemy of all righteousness, will you not cease perverting the straight ways of the Lord?"

> **(Acts 13:10)**

Elymas paraded himself as a prophet, but Paul called him a man "full of all deceit and all fraud." He called him a "son of the devil" and an "enemy of righteousness." There are many so-called "prophets" in the church today who mis-use their prophetic gifts to defraud people. They do this intentionally and blatantly. In the words of Paul, they are sons of the devil and enemies of righteousness!

Peter also had a similar encounter with a sorcerer, named Simon, when he ministered in Samaria. Simon was hailed by everyone in the city as "the great power of God." Everyone "heeded him because he had astonished them with his sorceries for a long time" (Acts 8:9-11). However, when the people turned to Christ in their numbers because of the preaching of Phillip, Simon also gave his life to Christ. He was amazed by the signs, wonders, and miracles that God was doing through the hands of Phillip.

Simon was astonished even more when he saw the people receiving the baptism of the Holy Spirit after Peter laid hands on them. He then offered Peter money so he could possess the same ability to make people speak in tongues. He saw the gospel as an opportunity to gain influence once again over people. He also reduced the ministry to a business transaction. Peter did not mince words when he confronted his error.

> *But Peter said to him, "Your money perish with you, because you thought that the gift of God could be purchased with money! You have neither part nor portion in this matter, **for your heart is not right in the sight of God.** Repent therefore of this your wickedness, and pray God if perhaps the thought of your heart may be forgiven you. For I see that you are poisoned by bitterness and bound by iniquity."*
>
> ### *(Acts 8:20-23)*

Unfortunately, the hearts of many who minister in the Lord's name are not right before God. They are more concerned about money, fame, ministerial accolades, and the praise of men. Even some who started well have derailed because of covetousness. Stories abound of people who sought power from dark sources and are using sorcery to keep people captive and extort them of their hard-earned cash. The average person cannot discern the difference between true and false miracles because these impostors have every appearance of a gospel minister, and they perform their wonders in the Lord's name. Surely, not everyone who does miracles in the Lord's name has the Lord's approval. The Bible says clearly that such men (and women) would increase in the last days and their deception will go from bad to worse. The evidence is all around us.

THE GOSPEL AND MONEY

Whenever the message of the cross of Jesus is mixed with an overemphasis on money, the mystery of iniquity might be lurking in the shadows. Many, through what has been called the "prosperity gospel," have subtly diluted the truths of God, reducing the gospel of Jesus to a transactional means to attaining a "better life." There are preachers today who consistently twist and manipulate God's word in order to deceive and defraud people. They promise their congregants God's blessings, but only in exchange for the people's gold and silver. The unsuspecting crowd are tricked to comply because the gimmick is done in the Lord's name.

Surely, prosperity is one of the benefits of our salvation, but it is not the *reason* for our salvation. Healing is one of the benefits of our salvation, but it is not the *reason* for our salvation. When money, directly or indirectly, becomes the focus of the gospel message, iniquity is not far away. The exponential increase in the way money has dominated the gospel message is a sign of the last days and a reason why the love of many has waxed cold. Uncountable numbers of believers have stopped going to church altogether, while others have switched to seemingly less-extorting traditional churches.

Paul said a bishop should not be "greedy for

money" (1 Timothy 3:3-4). Any minister who is greedy for money will consider the gospel of Jesus as "a source of profit [a lucrative, money-making business]" (1 Timothy 6:5 AMP). Instead of an over-emphasis on money, ministers need to demonstrate that "godliness with contentment is great gain," and that "we brought nothing into this world, and it is certain we can carry nothing out. And having food and clothing, with these we shall be content" (1 Timothy 6:6-8).

The fate of ministers who prioritise money over truth is clear:

> But those who desire to be rich **fall into temptation and a snare**, and into **many foolish and harmful lusts** which drown men in **destruction and perdition**. For the love of money is a root of **all kinds of evil**, for which some have strayed from the faith in their greediness, and **pierced themselves through with many sorrows**.
>
> **(1 Timothy 6:9-10)**

Paul, in this scripture, focused his admonition on ministers and their attitude to money. He instructed Timothy to "*flee these things* and pursue righteousness, godliness, faith, love, patience, gentleness" (1 Timothy 6:11). Through-out his ministry, Paul was careful not to taint the gospel he preached by abusing his authority over the people and their finance. Sadly, too many ministers are no longer careful. They do not *flee* from manipulative practices but embrace and use them unashamedly. Many have departed the faith for this reason.

SPIRITS OF DECEPTION AND DOCTRINES OF CONFUSION

*Now the Spirit expressly says that in latter times **some will depart from the faith**, giving heed to **deceiving spirits** and doctrines of demons, speaking lies in hypocrisy, having their own conscience seared with a hot iron.*

(I Timothy 4:1-2)

Alongside widespread sorcery, trickery, and extortion in the church of the last days, which would cause the love many to wax cold, there would also be an influx of deceiving spirits and questionable doctrines that will lead to a falling away of many from the faith. The Greek word *aphistemi*, translated "depart" in this scripture, means "to *cause* to depart" or "to *cause* to revolt." Hence, some will depart from the faith *because* they give attention to doctrines from hell.

We have noted already that unwholesome doctrines have been an issue of contention in the church from the first century. The Holy Spirit was warning that the impact would be more pronounced in the last days because the devil will focus his demonic forces on the promotion and propagation of deceptive doctrines. These demons would seek vessels through whom they can spread lies. Many of these vessels would be preachers and teachers of the gospel. For this reason, we need to take heed *what* we hear, *how* we hear, and *who* we give attention to. There are many who speak in the name of the Lord that do not have the heart of the Lord.

The truth of the gospel sets people free, but erroneous doctrines keep people in bondage. Even those who start well on a solid ground of truth can end up in the claws of deception if they do not take heed. Any doctrinal emphasis that deviates from the simplicity and Lordship of Christ is suspect. We need keen discernment in these last days.

From the middle of the twentieth century, a philosophical movement called *deconstruction-ism*, made popular by the works of the French Philosopher, Jacques Derrida, has sought to demonstrate that any given text has inherent contradictions.[1] Hence, the meaning associated with historical texts can change in time. Applying this school of thought to theological under-standing and interpretation of scripture has led many to question the validity of what Christians in the modern era believe about God and the faith. It is good to ask questions, but if the end goal of these questions is to challenge and reject the fundamental truths of the gospel, then one has become a victim of deceiving spirits. The goal of these spirits is to cause people to revolt against ancient truths and deviate from the standards of God. For example, people have twisted the Bible to make it conform to humanistic ideologies, claiming that same sex relationships are *now* acceptable to God.

God is not an author of confusion. Paul admonished ministers to "reject profane and old wives' fables," avoid "disputes and arguments over words," and steer clear of "idle babblings and contradictions of what is falsely called knowledge." Those who give their time to these unwholesome practices are in danger of straying concerning the faith (see 1 Timothy 4:7, 6:4,20-21).

COLD LOVE IN A COLD WORLD

When Paul said there would be a "falling away" before the return of Christ, the phrase is often applied, and rightly so, to a departure from the faith, obviously by those already in or associated with the faith. However, we need to consider the wider implication of the increase in iniquity. In other words, what would be the impact of the heightened manifestation of the mystery of iniquity in the world? Firstly, let us look at these words of Christ again.

> Because lawlessness is increased, the love of **most people** will grow cold.
>
> ### (Matthew 24:12 AMP)

Jesus did not specify who these "most people" would be, whether Jews, gentiles, or people in general. He also did not qualify what kind of love will grow cold. Of course, love for God is implied, but the increase in wickedness will dampen love in a broader sense (the love *of* God and love *for* God is the root of genuine human love). Love for God will surely plummet in the last days, but so will the love people have for fellow humans, for truth, and for life itself. Paul alluded to this in his letter to Timothy. Notice what he says about love in the last days:

> But know this, that **in the last days** perilous times will come: **For men will be lovers of themselves, lovers of money,** boasters, proud, blasphemers, disobedient to parents, unthankful, unholy, **unloving**, unforgiving, slanderers, without self-control, brutal, despisers of good, traitors, headstrong, haughty, **lovers of pleasure rather than lovers of God.**
>
> ### (2 Timothy 3:1-4)

The effect of an increase in love for self, money, and pleasure, coupled with a decrease in love for God and others, would be all manners of brutality, oppression, exploitation, and wickedness in the world. We are witnessing these things today. There are many despicable things that people are doing for money, fame, and pleasure. Kidnapping, ritual killing, child molestation, people trafficking, swindling, and rage are rife today. The love people have for decency and the commonwealth of humanity is waxing cold. As a resultant effect, there is an increase in the number of people battling with disillusion, depression, and feelings of despair.

FROM DELUSION TO DELUSION

On the one hand, we can say that we live in a fallen world, and those in the world have already fallen short of God's glory, and there can be no further "falling away." However, the scriptures reveal the dynamics of this fall and how the world will seemingly "fall" even further as the last days become gloomier. It all comes down to a decrease in man's love for truth and an increase in their love for lies.

Through Adam, mankind rejected the authority and laws of God. Yet, God continued to reach out in love, manifesting Himself and establishing His standards through vessels who embrace His laws and truth. Even when the wickedness of man was at its peak, He found Noah and etched out a redemption plan for man. Noah, a "preacher of righteousness" declared the counsel of God to his generation, but no one heeded him until the flood came, by which time it was too late. Afterwards, God set a covenant sign in the firmament, the rainbow, to remind Him of His commitment to man, and to communicate God's love and supremacy to man. Whenever a rainbow appears in the skies, it is fulfilling its mandate to show forth God's glory throughout all generations. Indeed, all of nature declares the awesomeness of God.

> *The heavens declare the glory of God; and the firmament shows His handiwork. Day unto day utters speech, and night unto night reveals knowledge.* **There is no speech nor language where their voice is not heard.** *Their line has gone out through all the earth, and their words to the end of the world.*
>
> ### *(Psalm 19:1-3)*

So, God has never ceased to make Himself known to man through nature. *"Since the creation of the world* His invisible attributes are clearly seen, *being understood by the things that are made,* even His eternal power and Godhead"* (Romans 1:19-20). However, people have consistently chosen to suppress this knowledge and deny the obvious truths of God.

The consequence of man's decision not to retain the knowledge of God or acknowledge His almightiness is dire. Three times in his letter to the Romans, Paul stated how God responded to man's rejection of His laws:

> "Therefore **God also gave them up to uncleanness**, in the lusts of their hearts, to dishonor their bodies among themselves... For this reason **God gave them up to vile passions**... And even as they did not like to retain God in their knowledge, **God gave them over to a debased mind**, to do those things which are not fitting."
>
> **(Romans 1:24,26,28)**

By suppressing the truths of God, and exchanging truth for lies, mankind has gone from delusion to delusion, *falling further away* from God and embracing outright rebellion against His authority. The result of this rebellion is idolatry, immorality, confused sexuality, and debased ideologies.

Not only are homosexuality and lesbianism now commonplace in our world today; boys are being taught falsely that they can *choose* to be girls, and girls can *choose* to be boys. As if this is not bad enough, children are handed the *right* to undergo the inconvenience of surgically changing their sex. Transgenderism is a sure manifestation of the "falling away" of humanity from the core values of godliness. To make matters worse, the world no longer recognises two genders, but as many gender combinations as possible! Kindergarten children are being exposed to explicitly sexual "educational" content and told they can do whatever they like with their bodies. The mystery of lawlessness is not relenting its efforts to wreck the moral fabric of the world.

WHEN INIQUITY ABOUNDS

As deception and lawlessness multiply, and love for God becomes colder than it has ever been, the fallen state of man can sometimes seem to be unredeemable. But nothing can be further from the truth. There is no one "too lost" that the love of God cannot redeem. There is no sin too despicable for God to forgive. When iniquity abounds, the grace of God abounds much more (Romans 5:20)! Anyone who calls on the name of the Lord shall encounter God's love, receive the free gift of salvation, and enjoy inner peace.

Those who already know God and thereafter make a conscious choice to abandon their faith in Him are treading on dangerous ground; they are thus aligning themselves with the lawless one, the son of perdition, who will, in time, come to an utter end.

8

UNVEILING THE LAWLESS ONE

The multifaceted operation of the mystery of iniquity that we examined in previous chapters, fuelled by deception and resulting in rebellion, are working in sync to cover the earth with lawlessness and create a conducive environment for the rise of the Antichrist. Paul said this man must come first before the return of Christ.

> Let no one deceive you by any means; for that Day will not come unless the falling away comes first, and the man of sin is revealed, the son of perdition."

(2 Thessalonians 2:3)

In this chapter, we will explore the characteristics of the Antichrist that Paul highlighted in our text and cross-reference them with what other scriptures have said about him, allowing scripture to explain scripture. Through these, we would get a better picture of the nature and mission of the Antichrist. (The main cross-reference scriptures, which most scholars refer to when discussing the Antichrist, are Daniel 7-8, where he is the "little horn," and Revelation 12-13, where he is "the beast" empowered by the dragon).

Moreover, as we go through these traits, we would see, once again, that the Antichrist is opposed to Christ and his nature is totally different from Christ's.

Man of sin

The first description Paul gave to the Antichrist in this scripture was "man of sin" (2 Thessalonians 2:3). By this, he meant sin, which is the transgression of God's law, would be the Antichrist's core identity - what he represents, what drives him, and what makes him who he is. Everything he does would be contrary to God's word and nature. Sin would be the Antichrist's natural disposition. He would be the epitome of transgression. None of the other scriptures that refer to the Antichrist attribute even an iota of righteous acts to him. They refer to him as pompous, dubious, and callous.

Christ, on the other hand, is the righteousness of God. He knew no sin but became sin in order that He might condemn sin in His body through death on the cross; that those who believe in Him are translated from death to life and become free from the penalty and power of sin. In these last days, people will identify themselves either with the man of sin or with the man of righteousness.

Son of perdition

Paul called the Antichrist, "the son of perdition" (2 Thessalonians 2:3). Jesus also used the phrase to refer to Judas Iscariot, the one who betrayed him after Satan had entered him (John 17:12). The word *perdition (apoleia)* means eternal ruin that is seemingly irreversible. Thus, the destiny of the Antichrist is clear: he is marked for complete and utter destruction in the end (see chapter 9). In Daniel's visions, the Antichrist will be consumed and destroyed forever (Daniel 7:26), and in Revelation, the beast will "go to perdition" (Revelation 17:8,11).

Christ, on the other hand, is the source of salvation. His name, Yeshua, means "to save" or salvation. The Antichrist comes to steal, kill, and ultimately destroy, but Jesus gives abundant life. Those who align themselves with "the son of perdition" will share in his irrevocable end, which is destruction. Those who align themselves with Yeshua will have life forevermore.

Opposes God

Paul went on to say that the Antichrist "opposes... all that is called God or that is worshipped" (2 Thessalonians 2:4). To *oppose* means "to stand against." Thus, the Antichrist will be directly and intentionally against anything that is God's, originates from God, or is attributable to God. He will attack it, stand against it, and work contrary to it. He will even clamp down on all forms of religious worship and oppose any allegiance people have to deity. According to one of Daniel's visions, "he shall speak pompous words *against* the Most High" (Daniel 7:25).

Christ was and is one with God. He loves the Father and is in perfect union with Him. He only did His Father's will and opposed those who misrepresented the Father's heart. Those who receive Christ also receive this love disposition towards God.

Exalts himself above God

Paul added that the Antichrist will "exalt himself above all that is called God" (2 Thessalonians 2:4). All the other scriptures state the same trait. He, the Antichrist, will "exalt himself as high as the Prince of the host... he shall exalt himself in his heart... he shall even rise against the Prince of princes" (Daniel 8:11,25). "He shall exalt and magnify himself above every god, shall speak blasphemies against the God of gods… He shall regard neither the God of his fathers nor the desire of women, nor regard any god; *for he shall exalt himself above them all*" (Daniel 11:36-37).

Contrast this with Christ "who, being in very nature God, did not consider equality with God something to be used to his own advantage; rather, he made himself nothing by taking the very nature of a servant" (see Philippians 2:5-9). Jesus humbled Himself and was consequently exalted to the highest place, but the Antichrist will arrogantly exalt himself and will be brought down to the lowest place.

Sits as God in the temple of God

We have noted earlier that the ambition of Lucifer from the beginning of time has been to ascend the throne of God (Isaiah 14:13). Paul revealed in his epistle that the Antichrist will "sit as God in the temple of God, showing himself that he is God" (2 Thessalonians 2:4). He will exalt himself as God "and by him the daily sacrifices" would be offered (Daniel 8:11, compare with Daniel 9:27). In short, he will demand that the peoples of the world worship him and the dragon that gave him power (Revelation 13:12). However, in the same way that Lucifer was cast down to the earth, he will again be cast down to the bottomless pit and the lake of fire (Revelation 19:20).

Jesus humbled Himself and obeyed the Father by laying down His life for man. As a result, He now sits at the right hand of the Father in glory. Those who believe in Him are also raised together with Him and sit with Him in heavenly places in Him (Ephesians 2:6).

Persecutes the saints

We have noted already how the mystery of iniquity operates in the persecution of the saints. Anyone who is vehemently and fundamentally opposed to God will also be opposed to God's people (John 15:18-20). The rule of the Antichrist will witness more antagonism toward the followers of Christ. He "shall persecute the saints of the Most High... destroy the mighty, and also the holy people" (Daniel 7:25, 8:24. See also Revelation 12:17).

Jesus is a reliable prayer partner of the saints. He is able to preserve them through seasons of persecution. In the same way that He faced and overcame death, He helps those who are persecuted to endure and overcome death by giving them grace to "not love their lives to the death" (Revelation 12:11). He taught His disciples not to fear those who can only kill the body and not the spirit (Matthew 10:28, Luke 12:4).

Before He ascended into heaven, not only did He assure us of His presence "till the end of the age," He also encouraged us to be of good cheer in the face of tribulation because He has overcome the world.

The lawless one

Paul, referring to the Antichrist, said "the lawless one will be revealed" (2 Thessalonians 2:8). This reference means that the Antichrist will show no regard for the laws of God. He will operate in total defiance to God's divine standards of morality and decency. Having exalted himself above all mankind and every deity, the Antichrist would revel in a false sense of almightiness. The angel who interpreted Daniel's vision said the Antichrist "shall intend to change times and law" (Daniel 7:25). Indeed, he "shall do according to his own will" (Daniel 11:36). In other words, he would be a law unto himself.

Jesus did not do anything of His own accord. He was subject to the Father and came to be the fulfilment of God's law. Although His death abolished the law of Moses, His resurrection established a new law of the Spirit, the law of love that fulfils every commandment. The Antichrist will not respect any law because he will consider himself "the law."

The handiwork of Satan

Paul said that "the coming of the lawless one is according to *the working of Satan*" (2 Thessalonians 2:9). That is, the rise of the Antichrist will be the direct manoeuvring of the devil. The world would see a man, but the old dragon would be the one working in and through the man. Referring to the beast that would rise out of the sea, John said "the dragon gave him *his power, his throne*, and great authority" (Revelation 13:2). The Antichrist's ability to do the things the scriptures say he would do, to the scale and extent to which he would do them, is because the devil will be his architect and source.

This is to directly rival Christ, who is the express image of the Father. Jesus was able to do the things that He did when He walked the earth because God was with Him, and God anointed Him. Everything about Christ, from His birth to His ascension, was the handiwork of God.

Power, signs, & lying wonders

Not only would the coming of the lawless one be the direct work of Satan; he would also come "with all power, signs, and lying wonders" (2 Thessalonians 2:9). Through the activities of an ally beast (see *Unholy Trinity* on page 140), the Antichrist will "perform great signs, so that he even makes fire come down from heaven on the earth in the sight of men" (Revelation 13:13). He will display spectacular miracles that would astonish the undiscerning.

> And I saw one of his heads as if it had been mortally wounded, and his deadly wound was healed. **And all the world marvelled and followed the beast.**
>
> **(Revelation 13:3)**

Jannes and Jambres were able to resist Moses for a season because of their ability to turn their rods into snakes, and water into blood (2 Timothy 3:8). Judged solely on their ability to manipulate the natural order, there was no clear distinction between Moses and the magicians of Egypt. And this is where the Antichrist is going to succeed in his ministry of deception, for many will not know how to discern between lying miracles that proceed from Satan and true miracles that are performed through God.

Miracles that are done for show and not for the glory of God, no matter the calibre of person who performs them, are questionable. Miracles are not the ultimate sign of God's acceptance. Of course, the Antichrist will seek to mirror the true Christ, whom God approved of "by miracles, wonders, and signs." The difference, however, is that the miracles of Christ are for the *freedom* of captives; the Antichrist's miracles are for the *binding* of captives.

Unrighteous deception

Paul went on to say that the "signs and lying wonders" that the Antichrist will perform will be done "with all *unrighteous deception* among those who perish" (2 Thessalonians 2:9). According to Daniel's vision, the Antichrist will understand "sinister schemes," and "through his cunning *he shall cause deceit to prosper under his rule*" (Daniel 8:25). Deception would be the order of the day when the Antichrist rises to power. Not only would he control the whole world through manipulation and deception; he would also suppress truth and *"cast truth down to the ground"* (Daniel 8:12). He would take charge of all public discourses and exercise control over every narrative about what is true and lawful. He will censor and prohibit any dissenting voice and make the whole world believe he is doing so for their good. The Antichrist will speak the devil's native language, which is lies.

Jesus Christ is the way, the truth, and the life. He came into the world to "bear witness to the truth," and everyone who is of the truth will hear His voice and reject the voice of the Antichrist (John 18:37).

UNHOLY TRINITY

The theme of the next two sections, although not directly stated by Paul in his letter to the

Thessalonians, are from the cross-reference book of Revelation, and helpful in completing our biblical understanding of the Antichrist's traits and reign. The first is the manifestation and co-working of an unholy trinity: the dragon, the beast, and the false prophet (Revelation 12 and 13), obviously mimicking the Godhead - the Father, Son, and Holy Spirit.

The dragon: The scriptures clearly state the identity of the dragon.

> So the great dragon was cast out, that serpent of old, **called the Devil and Satan**, who deceives the whole world.
>
> **(Revelation 12:9)**
>
> He laid hold of the dragon, that serpent of old, **who is the Devil and Satan...**
>
> **(Revelation 20:2)**

The devil is the mastermind of all the evil that will culminate during the Antichrist's era. As noted previously, he would directly empower the beast. The devil will give the Antichrist *"his power, his throne, and great authority"* (Revelation 13:2).

The beast: This would be a human being, a world ruler, someone who is fully inhabited and possessed by the devil. This would perhaps be the devil's best imitation of the incarnated Christ. Evidently, this best attempt will fall short on every account. The beast will have a deadly wound and subsequently appear healed (Revelation 13:3). Well, this cannot be compared with the resurrection of Christ from the dead!

Moreover, the beast, the Antichrist, will cause people to worship the dragon, the devil. He will accomplish this through deception, coercion, and threats. Jesus Christ, the true Saviour of mankind, would never force people to worship Him. He demonstrated the greatest form of love when He gave up His life for man's redemption on the cross of calvary. This love act of self-sacrifice alone draws mankind to worship God, not to talk about the resurrection from the dead that seals the eternal destiny of those who believe in Him.

The false prophet: To complete the devil's unholy trinity, the Bible reveals the rising of "another beast coming up out of the earth" (Revelation 13:11). This would likely be a religious leader of some sort, a self-proclaimed prophet, or a miracle -worker. So, we have the dragon (Satan), the first beast (the Antichrist), and the second beast (called the "false prophet" in Revelation 16:13 and 19:20). The false prophet will perform deceptive signs and wonders and will exercise the authority of the first beast.

Notice that the false prophet, called "another beast," a *heteros* or second beast, came up "out of the earth," whilst the Antichrist, the first beast, rose "up out of the sea" (Revelation 13:1). Is there any significance in these observations? Well, the Holy Spirit, whom Christ promised to send is "another comforter," an *allos parakletos*, who "proceeds from the Father" (see John 14:16,15:26). He is another comforter of the same kind as Christ, and He proceeded from the Father just as Christ did. Therefore, the unholy trinity of the dragon, the Antichrist, and the false prophet, a mere mish-mash of rebellious spirit and human entities, can never measure up to the glory, oneness, and holiness of the blessed Godhead - God the Father, God the Son, and God the Holy Spirit!

MARK OF THE BEAST

Now, there are a few primary assignments the false prophet is going to execute on behalf of the Antichrist (see Revelation 13:11-17):

- He will deceive those who dwell on the earth with his signs and lying miracles.

- He will instruct everyone to make and possess an image of the Antichrist. This image will come to life and demand that people worship the beast (the Antichrist).

- He will persecute and kill those who refuse to worship the beast or the image of the beast.

- He will cause all people, "both small and great, rich and poor, free and slave, *to*

> *receive a mark* on their on their right hand or
> on their foreheads."

- He will only allow those who have the
  mark of the beast to engage in commercial
  activities, like buying and selling.

We have already touched on the first three of
these assignments (deception and lying miracles;
call to worship; and persecution of those who
refuse to worship the beast). The final two tasks
relate to the administration of a mark on behalf
of the beast. But what is this much-talked-about
"mark of the beast"? Many have speculated as to
what it is and what form it would take.
Considering it in its full context would shed
further light on it.

Firstly, recall that the false prophet, the one
who would administer the mark on people, will
work for or form part of the Antichrist's global
government. He will demand that people worship
the Antichrist and prevent those who choose not
to from engaging in commercial activities. Here
we see a fusion of government, religion, and trade,
all combining as one global operation; and only a
certain calibre of people would be allowed to
operate within this economy: those who take the
mark of the beast. If a person refuses the mark, he
or she would not have access to the benefits
offered by the government of the beast, including
buying or selling essential items.

With the exponential advancements in digital technology, speculation about the mark of the beast have also increased, ranging from electronic barcodes to microchip implantation. It is widely speculated that a chip, or its equivalent, that contains the personal and financial information of each person will be inserted into the skin and be the medium for communication and economic transactions. This kind of sophisticated digital technology is around today and still developing.

We may not know for sure what form this mark would take. However, the *essence* of the mark might be of more critical importance than the *technology* of the mark. By focusing more on how the mark could be administered, we have, perhaps, not fully grasped what Jesus wanted us to understand about it.

The word interpreted as "mark" in Revelation 13:17-18 (and other chapters of the book) is *charagma*, which means "a stamp" or "an impress." The root word, *charasso*, means "to engrave." It bears similarity to the description given to Jesus Christ in Hebrews 1:3: "He reflects the glory of God and bears *the very stamp of his nature*" (RSV). The Amplified Bible says that Christ is "the exact representation *and perfect imprint of His [Father's] essence.*" In other words, to receive the mark of the beast means one becomes an imprint of the Antichrist's *personality.*

This becomes clearer when we consider how the scripture *defines* the mark. To *see* this, it is important we disregard the *technology* of the mark and focus on the *essence* of the mark:

> Also it causes all, both rich and poor, both free and slave, to be marked on the right hand or the forehead, so that no one can buy or sell **unless he has the mark, <u>that is,</u> the name of the beast or the number of its name.**
>
> ### (Revelation 13:16-17 RSV)

According to this scripture, the mark of the beast (or the essence of the mark) is not the barcode or the microchip; it is either of these two things: *the name* of the beast or *the number* of its name. When a person receives the mark of the beast, he or she receives an imprint of the beast's name and everything the name connotes - his character, authority, personality etc. The Antichrist's name or the number of his name (we would explore the number of the name in the last section) is more than the name he was given at birth or the collection of letters that spell his name; his name represents his essence and the totality of who he is. To bear an imprint of his name means one identifies with him and can be called his own.

The essence of the name of Jesus is not in the letters J-E-S-U-S or Y-E-S-H-U-A. His name represents all that He is: His power, glory, mission, authority, character, and deity. So, by entrusting His name to those who believe in Him, He is endowing them with all of Himself and all that He can do. By believing in the name of Jesus and receiving the authority to use His name, one becomes a representative of Jesus on the earth.

Those who receive the mark of the beast will also walk in a measure of the beast's authority and enjoy the privileges that the name gives, like the ability to buy and sell. Jesus has all authority in heaven and earth, so those who walk in the authority of His name will exercise dominion in both realms. But the Antichrist will *only* have temporary authority on the earth, and those who walk in his authority, because they have received his mark, will only exercise dominion on the temporal things of the earth, like buying and selling.

The technology of the mark might well involve a microchip or another biotechnological implant; it could have facial and hand recognition capabilities; it could give the bearer access rights to services that the Antichrist controls. Yet, receiving the mark means agreeing to all the Antichrist's terms and conditions, including outright rebellion against God and a commitment to worship the dragon and the beast's image. This will not be written in small print. It will be clear and obvious. No one can receive the mark of the beast by accident. The conditions would be evident. A person who chooses to receive the beast's mark, invariably and willingly, also embraces the agenda, philosophy, disposition, and character of the beast.

THE NUMBER OF THE BEAST

Now, if the mark of the beast is the Antichrist's name *or* the number of his name (Revelation 13:17 RSV), what does the latter signify? We have seen the significance of the beast's name, but what about his number? This has been the subject of much speculation amongst scholars; however, we need to consider it within the context of the discussion and examine it with understanding.

> *Here is wisdom. Let him who has understanding calculate the number of the beast, for it is the number of a man: His number is 666.*
>
> ### *(Revelation 13:18)*

Let us first make the following logical deductions from the texts. Revelation 13:17, which we previously explored, states that the mark of the beast *is* "the name of the beast *or* the number of his name." From this statement, we can deduce the following:

The *mark* of the beast *(a)*

= The *name* of the beast *(b)*

= The *number* of the beast's *name (c)*

That is, a = b = c (Equation 1).

From Revelation 13:18, quoted above, we can deduce the following:

The *number* of the *beast (d)*

= The *number* of a *man (e)*

= Six Hundred and Sixty-Six *(f)*

That is, d = e = f (Equation 2).

If the true essence of a *name*, as previously discussed, is the summation of the characteristics of the *person* bearing the name, then the following is also true:

The number of the beast's *name (c)*

= The number of the *beast (d)*

That is, c = d (Equation 1 = Equation 2).

Consequently, the following is true:

The mark of the beast *(a)*

= The name of the beast *(b)*

= The number of the beast's name *(c)*

= The number of the beast *(d)*

= The number of a man *(e)*

= Six Hundred and Sixty-Six *(f)*

Now, why go through the above logic and what is the point of this conclusion? First, to highlight a mistake that many scholars, through the generations, have possibly made in trying to identify the Antichrist using a lexicon and numeric formulae. Through a system called *Gematria*, one can assign numerical values to the letters of the name and compute them to find the supposed "number of the name." For instance, applying this formula to the wicked Roman Emperor, Nero Caesar (once thought of to be the Antichrist), his name adds up to the value 666. But so does the application to some other historic figures, like Muhammed and modern leaders, like Ronald Wilson Reagan! We miss the point if we get fixated only on the *number* of the beast, because the number *is* the name, and the name *is* the number. There is a more cogent reason why Jesus gave John these insights for the Church, much more than wanting us to correctly pinpoint the Antichrist. He wanted readers to gain understanding and walk in wisdom.

HERE IS WISDOM

Here is wisdom. Let him that hath understanding **count** *the number of the beast: for <u>it is</u> the number of a man; and his number is Six hundred threescore and six.*

(Revelation 13:18 KJV)

Jesus never intended for us to "calculate" the number of the beast's name. The Greek word *psephizo* is better translated as "count" and not "calculate". To *count* here means *to reckon, to vote, to decide*. It is the same word used in Luke 14:28, where the builder of a tower first "*counts* the cost" *before* deciding or voting to embark on his building project. In other words, we are enjoined to *count the cost* of identifying with the beast, knowing who he is and what he stands for, *because* he bears the number of a man, and the number is Six hundred and sixty-six.

The number of a man: Despite his pompous claims of being God, and his close partnership with the dragon, the Antichrist will still be a man - a man of perdition. Only Christ could correctly claim oneness with the true God when He walked the earth. He was fully God and fully man. The Antichrist would only be man, nothing more. When the people hailed king Herod and said, "The voice of a god and not of a man," he was immediately eaten by worms to show that he is only man and not God (see Acts 12:22-23).

Six Hundred and Sixty-Six: This point is further stressed in the true significance of the number 666. Many take a sensational approach to this number and associate it with the technology of the beast's mark. The truth is, six is the imperfect number of man—one short of seven, God's number of perfection. No matter how you scale imperfection, whether hundred-fold (600), ten-fold (60), or single-fold (6), it will only yield *perfect imperfection (666)*. This is the true significance of the number of the beast. The technology is a secondary matter.

IT IS TIME TO CHOOSE

The primary reason why we were asked to *count* the number of the beast (that is, his name, and who he represents) is so we can make an educated choice between Christ and the Antichrist, between the mark or name of the beast that leads to condemnation, and the name of Christ, the only name given unto man for salvation (Acts 4:12).

There are only two names on the ballot sheet of life; who are you going to vote for? You cannot be an undecided voter. There is no middle ground. Your name is either written in the Lamb's book of life or you are bound to receive the mark of the beast. Now that you have understanding, it is time for you to apply your heart to wisdom and decide. Also, if you have already chosen Christ, it is wise to help others make the right choice.

> *Those who are wise shall shine like the brightness of the firmament, and those who turn many to righteousness like the stars forever and ever.*

(Daniel 12:3)

9

ARMAGEDDON

Paul's focus in writing his second epistle to the Thessalonians was to dispel the idea that Christ had already returned to earth. He stated clearly that the Antichrist would come *first* and then the true Christ; and when Christ appears, the unrighteous regime of the man of lawlessness will come to an abrupt end.

> And then the lawless one will be revealed, **whom the Lord will consume with the breath of His mouth and destroy with the brightness of His coming.**
>
> **(2 Thessalonians 2:8)**

Other cross-reference scriptures also predict the fall of the Antichrist and his government.

> I was watching; and the same horn was making war against the saints, and prevailing against them, **until the Ancient of Days came,** and

> *a judgment was made in favor of the saints of the Most High, and the time came for the saints to possess the kingdom.*
>
> **(Daniel 7:21-22)**

> *And in the latter time of their kingdom, When the transgressors have reached their fullness, A king shall arise, having fierce features, who understands sinister schemes. His power shall be mighty, but not by his own power; he shall destroy fearfully, and shall prosper and thrive; he shall destroy the mighty, and also the holy people. Through his cunning he shall cause deceit to prosper under his rule; and he shall exalt himself in his heart. He shall destroy many in their prosperity. He shall even rise against the Prince of princes;* **But he shall be broken without human means.**
>
> **(Daniel 8:23-25)**

Despite all the devastation that the Antichrist will cause on the earth, "yet he shall come to his end, and no one will help him" (Daniel 11:45). The destiny of the Antichrist is unequivocal: he will go down in utter defeat as he attempts to rise against Christ, the Prince of peace.

So, when, according to Paul's letter, will the Antichrist's end come? At the coming of Christ. How will his end come? Through the breath of Christ's mouth and the brightness of His coming.

UNHOLY ALLIANCE

*And I saw three unclean spirits like frogs coming out of the mouth of the dragon, out of the mouth of the beast, and out of the mouth of the false prophet. For they are spirits of demons, performing signs, **which go out to the kings of the earth and of the whole world, to gather them to the battle of that great day of God Almighty.** "Behold, I am coming as a thief. Blessed is he who watches, and keeps his garments, lest he walk naked and they see his shame." **And they gathered them together to the place called in Hebrew, Armageddon.***

(Revelation 16:13-16)

The unholy trinity of the dragon, the Antichrist, and the false prophet are going to join forces to mobilise an alliance of nations against the Most High. In a sense, the devil will try to replicate on earth the war he waged and lost in heaven. He will send out demons and principalities to stir the hearts of national leaders to join in the battle.

And I saw the beast, the kings of the earth, and their armies, gathered together to make war against Him who sat on the horse and against Him army.

(Revelation 19:19)

THE FIG TREE?

According to John's vision, the nations will gather around the hills of *Megiddo*, known in Hebrew as *Armageddon*. In literal terms, Megiddo is situated in the northern region of modern Israel. This, perhaps, places a spotlight on Israel with regards to end-time events. Indeed, Israel, God's chosen land, and the Jews, God's chosen people, have always been an epicentre of prophecy. Observing developments in the region is akin to the *Fig Tree* approach that some have adopted to dissect end-time prophecies.

> *Now learn this parable from the fig tree: When its branch has already become tender and puts forth leaves, you know that summer is near. So you also, when you see all these things, know that it is near - at the doors!*

(Matthew 24:32-33)

In some prophetic books of the Bible, Israel and the Jewish people are often depicted as a fig tree (for example: Hosea 9:10; Joel 1:7; Jeremiah 24:1-6). The children of Israel belong to God by election, and God has set a divine agenda to redeem Israel again (see, for instance, Romans 11:25-32 in the context of the preceding chapters).

What happens to and in Israel has prophetic significance for the rest of the world. The historical contention for the land is a point in question, as well as the right of the Jews to exist as a people. The events of AD 70, when Jerusalem was burnt to the ground and the second temple destroyed are pivotal. As we have already seen, some scholars (preterists) believe these events fulfilled most, if not all of Christ's end-time predictions. Jesus had said, "When you see Jerusalem surrounded by armies, then know that its desolation is near" (Luke 21:20). This happened as the Roman armies ravaged the "Fig tree" and the Jews were permanently ejected from the land. However, in 1948, Israel was reconstituted as a sovereign nation, the "Fig tree" began to bud afresh, signifying that God had not finished with Israel. Would there be yet another gathering of nations against Israel?

The contention over the land persists and hostile nations, especially Iraq and the Hezbollah in Palestine, are bent on obliterating Israel from the face of the earth. If the Antichrist is opposed to God and God's people, then his regime will, most likely, be opposed to Israel, hence the mobilisation of nations against the nation and all that the nation represents.

WARS, RUMOURS OF WAR, AND THE FINAL WAR

Jesus said, "you will hear of wars and rumours of wars," meaning there would be wars within your regions and wars in regions beyond you that you would only hear about. With the globe as an inter-connected village, rumours of war now ring louder than they would have normally. Commotion in one region can readily impact other regions and threaten the fragile peace treaties that keep nations in check. In either case, even with the threat of a third global war, we should not be troubled "for all these things must come to pass, *but the end is not yet*" (Matthew 24:6).

Throughout history, kingdoms and nations have always been at war with one another. Conflicts abound for different reasons, including tussles over territory, resources, and ideology. There have been countless regional wars and two world wars. Of the fighting and conflict between men and nations, there shall be no end, until the Lord comes to put an end to all wars.

> Come, behold the works of the Lord, Who has made desolations in the earth. **He makes wars cease to the end of the earth;** He breaks the bow and cuts the spear in two; He burns the chariot in the fire.
>
> **(Psalms 46:8-9)**

In other words, there would be a final war, a desolation that the Lord will bring about in the earth, after which wars will cease. Could this final war be the one waged in the Megiddo valley, when Christ would defeat the dragon, the Antichrist, the false prophet, and all the kings of the earth that align with them?

CHRIST WINS IN THE END!

And I saw the beast, the kings of the earth, and their armies, gathered together to make war against Him who sat on the horse and against His army. **Then the beast was captured, and with him the false prophet who worked signs in his presence,** *by which he deceived those who received the mark of the beast and those who worshiped his image.* **These two were cast alive into the lake of fire burning with brimstone.** *And the rest were killed with the sword which proceeded from the mouth of Him who sat on the horse. And all the birds were filled with their flesh.*

(Revelation 19:19-21)

So, according to Paul's letter, and the witness from the book of Revelation quoted above, the Lord will consume the devil and his cohort "with the breath of His mouth and... the brightness of His coming." Hallelujah! God's righteous kingdom prevails in the end!

Maranatha, come Lord Jesus!

10

GOD RULES IN THE AFFAIRS OF MEN

In the concluding two chapters of this book, I want to highlight an important truth: that the sovereign God is in control of all that is happening on earth, and because He is in control, we need not be troubled or afraid - *no matter what happens on earth.* This, as we have seen, was one of the reasons Paul wrote to the Thessalonians; he did not want the believers to be "shaken in mind or troubled" because God oversees the sequence of end-time events (2 Thessalonians 2:2).

DELEGATED AUTHORITY

According to God's prophetic word, which we have briefly explored in this book, the government of the Antichrist will one day arise through deception and trickery. It will have global reach and control the world's economic, social, and religious systems. The administration will promote lawlessness, give special privileges to people who receive its mark, and persecute those who stand for godliness. It will be a government founded on lies, injustice, and oppression. Emboldened by a sense of absolute authority, the Antichrist and his allies will provoke the God of heaven, and thus meet their end. The scriptures, as we have seen, have predicted all these events.

Now, the Bible says, "there is no authority *except from God*, and the authorities that exist are *appointed by God*" (Romans 13:1). All earthly governments, the good, the bad, and the ugly, operate as God's appointees. They all function in the permissive will of God. They may not all be *good* or *perfect,* but they all, including the government of the man of lawlessness, have a licence to exercise delegated authority within their domain. The Antichrist, too, will rise to power, not because evil finally overpowers the forces of good, but because God will *allow* evil one final season of prominence. This evil regime will only see the light of day because God, in His time, so wills.

Throughout the generations of man's rebellion, God has been patient, and His patience will run its course so that even more people can get saved (2 Peter 3:9). Afterwards, He will allow the devil to operate for a season in delegated authority.

However, He will conquer and judge evil at the coming of Christ.

It is worth repeating that God is sovereign. The earth and its fullness are His. The world and its peoples are His. The governments of the world function under His jurisdiction with delegated authority. Even the Antichrist cannot exercise global dictatorship if the One who is restraining his rise does not allow it (see chapter 3).

Consider these verses and gain wisdom about this matter. This long text is worth reading. Notice the highlighted portions that show God's sovereignty over the affairs of the earth.

> *The beast that you saw was, and is not, and will ascend out of the bottomless pit and go to perdition. And those who dwell on the earth will marvel, whose names are not written in the Book of Life from the foundation of the world, when they see the beast that was, and is not, and yet is. "Here is the mind which has wisdom: The seven heads are seven mountains on which the woman sits. There are also seven kings. Five have fallen, one is, and the other has not yet come. And when he comes, **he must continue a short time.** The beast that was, and is not, is himself also the eighth, and is of the seven, and is going to perdition. "The ten horns which you saw are ten kings who have received no kingdom as yet, **but they receive authority for one** hour as kings with the*

*beast. These are of one mind, and they will give their power and authority to the beast. These will make war with the Lamb, and the Lamb will overcome them, for He is Lord of Lords and King of kings; and those who are with Him are called, chosen, and faithful." Then he said to me, "The waters which you saw, where the harlot sits, are peoples, multitudes, nations, and tongues. And the ten horns which you saw on the beast, these will hate the harlot, make her desolate and naked, eat her flesh and burn her with fire. **For God has put it into their hearts to fulfill His purpose, to be of one mind, and to give their kingdom to the beast, until the words of God are fulfilled.***

(Revelation 17:8-17)

God will put it into the hearts of the allied nations to give their delegated authority to the beast, which is the only way the Antichrist will possess absolute authority over the world's kingdoms. God will do this "to fulfil His purpose" and His word. Ultimately, He is in control.

When Pilate sat on the seat of judgement to sentence Christ, he thought he was in control of Christ's destiny. But Jesus corrected his assumption. Jesus told him, "You could have no power at all against Me *unless it had been given you from above*" (John 19:11). Similarly, the Antichrist would have no power at all if it were not handed over to him; and God will put it into the hearts of the nations to do just that - they will give their authority to the beast.

THE NEBUCHADNEZZAR SAGA

I want to emphasise the truth about God's sovereignty over human governments through the story of Nebuchadnezzar, king of Babylon, who reigned over many regions from 606-562 BC. Although he was a pagan king, thrice God called him "My servant" (see Jeremiah 25:9, 27:6, 43:10). God called him so because through him, some prophetic events would come to pass, including the captivity of Judah and the exile of the Jews from the promised land. As a king over a domain, Nebuchadnezzar operated in the permissive will of God as God's minister. He did not need to be good or perfect; he only needed to occupy that space, work in delegated authority, and fulfil God's purpose.

God needed a "servant" in Nebuchadnezzar when He wanted to send Israel into exile. He also needed a "servant" in king Cyrus, who ruled over Persia from 559-530 BC, to facilitate the return of the Jews from exile (see Ezra 1:1-11). Cyrus was a gentle, idol-worshipping king, but God called him to accomplish a prophetic purpose, making mention of him decades before he rose to power (Isaiah 44:28, 45:1).

King Nebuchadnezzar had a dream that none of his wise men could interpret. He had been thinking about what would happen in the world after he passed on, and God, responding to his query, gave him a startling dream (Daniel 2:29). Unsurprisingly, the wizards and magicians of Babylon could not recount the king's dream; they did not have access to the One who gave him the dream. But Daniel, an exiled youth from Judah, was a devoted worshiper of God. He prayed to God, and God gave him both the dream and the interpretation of the dream (he slept and had the same dream, essentially).

We will not explore the details and eschatological significance of Nebuchadnezzar's Dream (this is the focus of what I called the *Empire Prominence* approach to understanding end-time events). However, there are some things Daniel told the king that underscore the sovereignty of God over the history and destiny of mankind, especially human governments.

First, Daniel laid out the truth we are establishing in this discussion; that the vast authority Nebuchadnezzar had over the nations of the earth, including his conquest of Judah, was given to him by God.

> *You, O king, are a king of kings.* **For the God of heaven has given you a kingdom**, *power, strength, and glory; and wherever the*

*children of men dwell, or the beasts of the field and the birds of the heaven, **He has given them into your hand**, and has made you ruler over them all—you are this head of gold.*

(Daniel 2:37-38)

Secondly, God oversees the succession of kings and kingdoms. He rules over, is aware of, and is involved in the rising and falling of kingdoms, from the greatest to the least.

*But after you shall arise **another kingdom** inferior to yours; then another, **a third kingdom** of bronze, which shall rule over all the earth. **And the fourth kingdom** shall be as strong as iron, inasmuch as iron breaks in pieces and shatters everything; and like iron that crushes, that kingdom will break in pieces and crush all the others.*

(Daniel 2:39-40)

God foretold the rise and fall of the Persian, Grecian, Roman, and allied kingdoms. Of course, He is sovereign over all the nations in between as well. The only kingdom that would rise and never fall is the one "cut out of the mountain without hands," His kingdom, which will stand forever (Daniel 2:45).

Thirdly, the understanding Daniel gained from this dream made him worship God as the One who *"removes kings and raises up kings"* (Daniel 2:21).

Inspired by this dream, Nebuchadnezzar's heart began to swell with pride. He built an image of gold and required all people to worship the image or get thrown into the fire. Daniel's three friends defied the king's decree and were condemned to death, but God rescued them from the fiery furnace — demonstrating that sometimes, God does not deliver us *from* tribulation fires, but sees us *through* them (Daniel 3).

This, of course, astounded Nebuchadnezzar, but it did not completely deliver him from the pride and arrogance that filled his heart. It took another troubling dream, Daniel's interpretation of the dream, and the eventual fulfilment of the dream for the message to finally get through to Nebuchadnezzar, that God is the possessor of all authority and all kings function in delegated authority. Those that venture beyond the boundaries of God's permissive will are setting themselves up to be dethroned. King Saul learnt the lesson too late; he strayed out of the parameters of God's permissive will for him, and God decided to replace him as king over Israel (see 1 Samuel 13:13-14). It was nearly too late for Nebuchadnezzar!

Between the time the king had his dream, to when he lost his mind and lived like a wild animal, to when his mind and kingdom were restored to him, a particular declaration was made three times that further reinforces the premise of this chapter. First, Nebuchadnezzar heard this statement in his dream:

> 'This decision is by the decree of the watchers,
> And the sentence by the word of the holy ones,
> In order that the living may know that **the Most High rules in the kingdom of men,** Gives it to whomever He will, And sets over it the lowest of men.'

(Daniel 4:17)

In his interpretation of the dream, Daniel said to Nebuchadnezzar:

> They shall drive you from men, your dwelling shall be with the beasts of the field, and they shall make you eat grass like oxen. They shall wet you with the dew of heaven, and seven times shall pass over you, till you know that **the Most High rules in the kingdom of men**, and gives it to whomever He chooses.

(Daniel 4:25)

Twelve months after Nebuchadnezzar heard the interpretation of his dream, his heart was once again lifted up in pride. He thought in his heart and spoke with his mouth the following words: "Is not this great Babylon, that I have built for a royal dwelling by my mighty power and for the honor of my majesty?" (Daniel 4:30). Moments after this prideful statement, God spoke from heaven:

> *While the word was still in the king's mouth, a voice fell from heaven: "King Nebuchadnezzar, to you it is spoken: the kingdom has departed from you! And they shall drive you from men, and your dwelling shall be with the beasts of the field. They shall make you eat grass like oxen; and seven times shall pass over you, until you know that **the Most High rules in the kingdom of men**, and gives it to whomever He chooses."*
>
> **(Daniel 4:31-32)**

This Nebuchadnezzar Saga establishes the eternal truth that God rules in the affairs of men, including the affairs of all nations in these last days. All kings rule by God's permission. When they promote lawlessness and injustice, the saints might have to endure some heat, and literally go through fire like Shadrach, Meshach, and Abednego did, or the lion's den like Daniel did, but God knows how to preserve His own. He also retains the right to remove and install kings. As this Babylonian king testified, all the works of our sovereign God are truth "and His ways justice. And those who walk in pride He is able to put down" (Daniel 4:37).

THE DONALD TRUMP SAGA

To conclude this chapter, I want to briefly discuss the subject of God's sovereignty over human governments as demonstrated in the forty-fifth presidency of the United States of America, which was occupied by Mr Donald Trump. But why talk about America and Donald Trump in a book about the end times and a discussion about God's sovereignty?

Firstly, the Donald Trump saga depicts, in modern-day terms, the rulership of God in the affairs of men. It can be instructive for us to see the truth about God's sovereignty not only played out in scripture, but also in our time. Secondly, there are lessons for the church of Jesus to learn about the involvement of God (or the church) in Donald Trump's presidency, especially considering the "failed" prophecies about his intended second term in office. Thirdly, it highlights, perhaps, the significance of America in the unfolding of end-time events (or, at least, it asks the question whether there is any such significance).

Let me mention upfront, that I am not drawing any prophetic parallel between Donald Trump and Nebuchadnezzar. I only want to show that God, even in the twenty-first century, still rules in the political arenas of this world.

Before Donald Trump announced that he would run for presidency in the 2016 elections, there were many prophecies about his rise to power, some as early as 2015.[1] But why would God be interested in the American presidency?

The United States of America is a global power nation considered to be the leader of the *free world*. Trade between nations is carried out in US dollars and governments hold the currency in their foreign exchange reserves for trade purposes. The US military, for many decades, has assumed the role of "global police," making lots of enemies in the process. The truth is, if there would be a centralised, global government, it would invariably involve America alongside other global agencies and the dominance of America in global affairs would have to be curtailed significantly. Concerted efforts to weaken America's economic and military standing amongst the comity of nations were seemingly playing out already and a potential Donald Trump presidency, it was perceived by some, would put a clog in the wheels of this agenda.

Against many odds, Donald Trump, a man with no political precedence, became president of the United States, fulfilling the prophecies that some had previously delivered. Thus, according to what we established earlier; he became God's "servant" by virtue of the office he occupied. He might have been unorthodox in the way he executed his presidential duties, but he did accomplish some notable feats, some that one might say have prophetic significance, including the recognition of Jerusalem as Israel's capital and the Abraham Accord peace treaty with some Arab nations.[2] Evidently, God had some things in mind He wanted to achieve through the Trump administration.

Perhaps, the most important "achievement" was the way he inadvertently exposed the mysterious political mechanism that seemed to operate secretly, away from common view, for the sole purpose of weakening American society from within and without. Deception, aggression, intimidation, blackmail, and manipulation, all seemed to come to the fore as his presidency came under constant attack. Donald Trump was bent on taking America on a path contrary to the globalisation agenda that undermined the country's upward trajectory in economic and military terms, but mainstream media and social media giants joined in the relentless attacks, which intensified during the covid-19 pandemic. Trump was also at loggerheads with NATO[3], WHO[4], WTO[5], and other global parastatals. For some, this is only American politics; but for the discerning, more was (and perhaps is) at play.

LESSONS FROM THE "FAILED" TRUMP PROPHECIES

So, God raised Donald Trump for a purpose. Not only did his involvement in the political arena bring the mystery of iniquity functioning in high places to light, sections of the church in America also became more politically and spiritually aware. There was a heightened desire to push against the tide of supposed evil that was gradually engulfing the nation, and Donald Trump was regarded as one ordained of God to *restrain* those who have globalist intentions and want to drag America down to realise these plans.

Donald Trump became, for many, the "saviour" of America's destiny, the defender of American rights and freedoms (and that of the free world), and the symbol of American patriotism. Even the evangelical church, directly or indirectly, embraced Trump as a God-sent, a "Cyrus" of our time. Evidently, many in the prophetic community put Trump on a high pedestal, and there were many prophetic declarations predicting victory in the 2020 presidential elections and a second, *consecutive,* Donald Trump presidency.

However, as Daniel stated clearly, God can *raise* kings and *remove* kings (Daniel 2:21). He rules in the affairs of men, and His righteous government is sovereign over every human government. He *raised* Donald Trump and *removed* Donald Trump. He might have used Donald Trump's presidency to bring many questionable, behind-the-scenes, cabal-driven forces to light, but was it God's intention to overcome these forces through Trump? Does God have an agenda to *prevent* a global government, and does He need Donald Trump to accomplish this? Would this not conflict with what we have unravelled so far from God's word, that the Antichrist's regime will emerge followed by the coming of Christ? Surely, Donald Trump is *not* the Christ that will overcome the Antichrist with the breath of His mouth and the brightness of His coming. I think the prophets crossed the line and began to declare what they would want to see happen and not *precisely* what God said would happen.

It is akin to what Jeremiah experienced in his day. Prophetically, he could clearly see the devastation that was about to befall Judah, and realised, painfully, that neither prophecies nor repentance could prevent what was coming. He thought about these inevitable things, and said "the priests shall be astonished, and the prophets shall wonder" (Jeremiah 4:9). Why would the priests be astonished, and the prophets wonder? Because many of them wanted their nation to prosper and were declaring "peace" over the nation as the word of the Lord. This, surely, was God's will because the Psalms encourage us to pray for the peace of Jerusalem! But Jeremiah understood differently. His prophecies went against popular judgement. Noticing how eagerly the prophets were prophesying peace, he even exclaimed, "Ah, Lord God! Surely *You have greatly deceived this people* and Jerusalem, saying, 'You shall have peace,' whereas the sword reaches to the heart" (Jeremiah 4:10). God did not deceive the people; the prophets were just not precise enough.

We are also living in a crucial season in history, and prophetic people need to be careful with their prophetic voice. When do we cross the line from declaring the mind of God to prophesying what *we* want to see? How do we know the difference? When Daniel interpreted Nebuchadnezzar's dream, he displayed brokenness mixed with precise wisdom in his delivery. He loved the king and would have wanted the dream to "concern those who hate" the king (Daniel 4:19); yet, Daniel had the courage and authority to not only deliver the message of the Lord, but also to demand that the king repent and embrace righteousness, "perhaps there might be a lengthening of your prosperity" (Daniel 4:26-27). Unfortunately, Nebuchadnezzar continued in pride and the Lord dealt with him. Did Trump display pride and arrogance during his time in office, and did the prophets get the message of the Lord about humility across to him?

These last days will require the Church to walk in a greater level of prophetic precision.

There is no power in prophesying a populist message just because others are declaring the same thing. We need to be like Micaiah, who prophesied a word that conflicted with popular prophetic opinion (see 1 Kings 22). If we do not rise to this level of prophetic sharpness, we might become susceptible to the influence of "lying spirits."

We need the precision and relevance of Agabus, who "stood up and showed by the Spirit that there was going to be a great famine throughout all the world" (Acts 13:27-18). This precise prediction helped the church to prepare strategically, practically, and decisively for what eventually occurred. We are currently facing a variety of tribulations, and more will inevitably befall the world. The Holy Spirit is committed to showing us things to come (John 16:13), and with the prophetic operating on this level, we can successfully navigate these times.

We also need the humility and discernment of David, who, when faced with the same enemy he had previously defeated (the Philistine army), in the same location he had previously experienced victory (the Valley of Rephaim), did not attack presumptuously. He asked God whether he should go up against them or not. God said he should not attack directly and gave him a different warfare strategy. Was it presumptuous to think that prophecies that came to pass in 2016 would similarly come to pass in 2020 just because the circumstances were identical? These are important lessons for a crucial time in history.

Finally, and by way of emphasis, God rules in the affairs of men. He is not a politician, but He rules over human politics. He is not a Democrat or a Republican; He does not identify with Labour over Conservative; He does not carry a PDP or an APC voting card. In short, He does not belong to any political party that occupies the political space in your nation. He is God over *all*. When Joshua asked the angel on who's side he was, Israel's or their adversary's, the angel said, "*No*, but as Commander of the army of the Lord I have now come" (Joshua 5:14). We cannot make the Lord take sides; we must be on *His* side — with Christ, in Christ, and for Christ.

We are living in a time of prophetic fulfilment. When the coming of the Antichrist's global government draws near, would our prophecies be able to prevent it? Of course, we should not just roll over and allow lawlessness to cover the earth. We should continue shining the light of the gospel of Jesus brightly in the world and rescuing as many as possible from an eternity without God. Ultimately, our times are in His hands, including the destiny of planet earth.

11

STAND TO THE END

Paul's intention in writing this portion of his letter was clear from the onset. He wanted to affirm the truth about Christ's coming and the church's gathering to the Lord and refute the false claims that Christ had already come. He wanted the believers to be grounded in truth and have the capacity to withstand erroneous doctrines purported by impersonating teachers. Being rooted in the truth about Christ's coming (and in the truth about our faith) guards the heart and mind against apprehension, anxiety, and confusion.

Paul then, in strong terms, warned against deception and stated categorically that Christ will come *after* the man of sin has been revealed and there has been a falling away from the truth. He elaborated on the nature of the man of sin, and the punishment awaiting him and those who align themselves with him. He also acknowledged the sovereignty of God over all governments, all seasons, and all mankind.

TWO PATHWAYS, TWO DESTINATIONS

There are two pathways in life that lead in opposite directions to contrasting, eternal destinations. One pathway, the mystery of lawlessness, is characterised by strong delusion and ends in condemnation.

> *And for this reason God will send them strong delusion, that they should believe the lie, **that they all may be condemned** who did not believe the truth but had pleasure in unrighteousness.*
>
> **(2 Thessalonians 2:11-12)**

The second pathway, the mystery of godliness, is characterised by divine convictions and ends in "the glory of our Lord Jesus Christ."

> *But we are bound to give thanks to God always for you, brethren beloved by the Lord, because God from the beginning **chose you for salvation** through sanctification by the Spirit and belief in the truth, to which He called you by our gospel, for **the obtaining of the glory of our Lord Jesus Christ.***
>
> **(2 Thessalonians 2:13-14)**

· It matters which path one is travelling on. Those on the lawlessness pathway will end up taking the mark of the beast and thus, perish with the beast when the Lord comes. Those on the godliness pathway have their names written in the Lamb's book of life and will be caught up to meet the Lord when He comes.

It matters which pathway you have chosen, and it is not too late to choose Christ and reject the Antichrist! When you choose Christ, you will discover that "God from the beginning *chose you for salvation* through sanctification by the Spirit and belief in the truth." If you are yet to, it is time you say *yes* to Christ.

TWO CONCLUDING ADMONITIONS

We will now conclude this eschatological discourse with the two admonitions Paul gave to the Thessalonians at the end of his letter: *stand fast* and *hold the traditions*; as well as the benedictory prayer he offered on their behalf.

Stand fast

The Greek word that Paul used for *stand* here is *steko*. It means to *stand upright* or *stand fast*. In this context, it means to stand fast in the teachings of the apostles and not to deviate from the truths of the gospel. This presupposes that one has already learnt apostolic doctrines. Thus, once learnt, the believer should stand firmly in them, rooted, and grounded in all that they have been taught by word, letter, and lifestyle. Believers today need to thoroughly learn and comprehend the foundational, scriptural doctrines "once for all delivered to the saints." Such understanding helps to sharpen one's discernment and guard against deception.

Standing fast in truth also requires personal conviction, which comes not just by hearing a teaching, but taking the time to personally verify the truth of what is taught. This was the culture of the Berean believers, one that all believers need to emulate.

> *These were more fair-minded than those in Thessalonica, in that they received the word with all readiness, and* **searched the Scriptures daily to find out whether these things were so***.*
>
> *(Acts 17:11)*

We need to test all things, including revelations, prophecies, and doctrines, and hold fast to only what is good (1 Thessalonians 5:21).

Hold the traditions

The second admonition Paul gave the believers was that they should "*hold the traditions* which you were taught whether by word or our epistle" (2 Thessalonians 2:15). This instruction goes together with the counsel to stand firm. In other words, the saints are to stand firm *by* "holding the traditions" they have been taught.

The Greek word, *paradosis*, translated *traditions*, means that which is "handed down," and used in this context, refers to the teachings of the apostles. Also, the traditions refer to how the teachings require us to conduct ourselves (see 1 Corinthians 11:2, 2 Thessalonians 3:6). This is distinct from the touch-not-eat-not traditions of the pharisees, which are not based on divine revelation from or interpretation of God's word, but on man's opinions and made-up customs. Such traditions, characterised by laws, rules, and restrictive regulations, are void of transformative power, and render the word of God ineffective (see Matthew 15:1-6).

Based on an understanding of Christian doctrine, the records in the books of Acts, and documented church history, some of the Christian traditions we need to hold dear, no matter what season we are in, include traditions founded on truth: traditions of grace, traditions of love, traditions of community, traditions of righteous living, and traditions of Spirit-led living.

PAUL'S BENEDICTORY PRAYER

To round up the discussion about the coming of Christ, the gathering up of the saints, the rise of the Antichrist, the mystery of lawlessness, and the One who is restraining its manifestation, Paul, as he normally does in all his epistles, prayed for his readers. This prayer is appropriate even today.

> *Now may our Lord Jesus Christ Himself, and our God and Father, who has loved us and given us everlasting consolation and good hope by grace, comfort your hearts and establish you in every good word and work.*

(2 Thessalonians 2:16-17)

This benedictory prayer encapsulates and reveals how the Godhead works together to guard, guide, sustain, and empower us through the turbulence of these last days.

God, the Father, because of His deep love for us (*agapao*), has given us everlasting consolation (*paraklesis*) and good hope (*elpis*) by grace (*charis*). In other words, God's love has equipped us to face any situation in the present and secured us for all eternity. God loves us and will never forsake us. He has given us *everlasting consolation*, which is consistent, ever-present encouragement through the Holy Spirit, our *Parakletos*, especially for when life gets unbearable in the present. He has also given us *good hope* for the future, a living hope that cannot disappoint or leave us ashamed. This hope is in Christ, the One who was, who is, and who is to come. It causes us to live with the consciousness of eternal reward, knowing that temporal comforts of this life cannot compare with the glory to come.

Moreover, Christ, the Son, will comfort our hearts through the Holy Spirit, our Comforter, and establish us in every good *word* and *work*. This means, until the Lord comes, we need to continue *testifying* to the lordship of Christ and *engaging* in the works God has entrusted into our hands. We are not meant to hide in caves, fearing what the Antichrist is scheming against the church. Rather, we need to occupy until the Lord comes and engage in good works that will bring glory to Him and draw people to His kingdom.

> *Therefore, my beloved, brethren, be steadfast, immovable, always abounding in the work of the Lord, knowing that your labour is not in vain in the Lord.*
>
> **(I Corinthians 15:58)**

POSTSCRIPT

I made a point at the beginning of this book that my goal in writing this book was not to answer *every* eschatological question that people have. Also, in keeping to the verse-by-verse exposition of 2 Thessalonians 2, I deliberately resisted the temptation to highlight, mention, or elaborately expound *every* appearance of the mystery of iniquity in our day and time. It is my belief that a firm understanding of what the Bible has revealed about this phenomenon would not only help readers to evaluate their end-time convictions, but also accurately discern events happening in the world around them.

Therefore, with this book as a biblical basis, others might consider it necessary to address specific issues or areas of interest, explain them more fully, and present useful knowledge that will benefit believers living in the end of time.

- Tokunbo Emmanuel

APPENDIX 1

THE NICENE CREED

We believe in one God, the Father, the Almighty, maker of heaven and earth, of all that is, seen and unseen. We believe in one Lord, Jesus Christ, the only Son of God, eternally begotten of the Father, God from God, Light from Light, true God from true God, begotten, not made, of one Being with the Father. Through him all things were made.

For us and for our salvation He came down from heaven: by the power of the Holy Spirit, He became incarnate from the Virgin Mary, and was made man. For our sake He was crucified under Pontius Pilate; He suffered death and was buried. On the third day He rose again in accordance with the Scriptures; He ascended into heaven and is seated at the right hand of the Father. He will come again in glory to judge the living and the dead, and His kingdom will have no end.

We believe in the Holy Spirit, the Lord, the giver of life, who proceeds from the Father and the Son. With the Father and the Son, He is worshipped and *glorified. He has spoken through the Prophets. We believe in one holy catholic* and apostolic Church. We acknowledge one baptism for the forgiveness of sins. We look for the resurrection of the dead, and the life of the world to come. Amen.*

*Catholic, meaning universal.

APPENDIX 2

RESOLVING ESCHATOLOGICAL CONFLICTS

The goal of this book was not to prove the correctness of one eschatological position over the other. Evidently, believers around the world, depending on geographical region, denominational affiliation, or theological understanding, have different views about the interpretation of end-time prophecies.

For instance, one of the conflicting viewpoints among Christians is the *timing* of Christ's coming and the gathering of the saints (popularly called the rapture) vis-a-vis the presumed seven-year Great Tribulation. In a survey conducted among believers, out of 207 respondents, 54.6% held the position that Christ will come *before* the Great Tribulation; 11.6% believed the church will be caught up in the *middle* of the Great Tribulation; 5.3% believed the Christ would come *after* the seven-year Great Tribulation; 14.5% were not sure; 8.6% held no position; and 1.9% believed the Great Tribulation has occurred already!

So, how do we resolve these conflicting positions and beliefs?

First, by acknowledging that eschatological positions are not fundamental to our salvation. Knowledge of and faith in the death and resurrection of Jesus Christ on the cross, and His precious blood that ratifies the new covenant are the things that are foundational, indispensable, and non-negotiable. On the correctness of these truths, there is little room for conflicting opinions. Whereas, on the timing of Christ's coming, one person might believe in one way and another person might believe in another way, according to their faith and theological influences. Yet, both remain in Christ because eschatological understanding is not the prerequisite to salvation; faith in the *finished work* of Christ on the cross is.

Secondly, by receiving one another despite our theological differences. Paul encouraged believers to receive one another and not resort to "disputes over *doubtful things*" (Romans 14:1). Evidently, eschatological persuasions are one of these "doubtful things." Applying this principle for resolving theological conflicts, let not him who believes one thing despise him who believes another thing, and let not him who does one thing because of what he believes judge the person who does another thing because of what he believes, for God has received both (Romans 14:3). Whichever way one believes, "let each be fully convinced in his own mind" (Romans 14:5).

Thirdly, we resolve these conflicting positions by focusing on Christ and His body. This means prioritising love that builds up the body of Christ over knowledge that puffs up the individual professor of truth. We should not attack one another and "destroy the work of God for the sake of" what we believe (Romans 14:20). Instead, we should "pursue the things which make for peace and the *things by which one may edify another*" (Romans 14:19). We are all baptised into Christ because of our love *for* and faith *in* Him, not because of our theological knowledge *about* Him.

Fourthly, by recognising the place of healthy debate. We can proactively engage in discussions and debates to look into the merits of different positions and learn from one another. When done in an attitude of respect, openness, and brotherly love, this can be very beneficial, especially on an apostolic level. The apostolic council convened by the leaders of the church in Jerusalem to discuss the subject of circumcision and the new creation (see Acts 15), as well as the numerous leadership councils throughout church history (like the Nicene Council), are examples of such engagements. Believers can also share with one another, not to castigate or put down one another, but to learn from one another.

Fifthly, by knowing that these conflicts will be resolved in time and in Christ. We are growing into Him in all things, and as we continue to edify one another, especially through the ministry gifts that Christ has set in the body, we "grow up in all things into Him who is the head" (see Ephesians 4:11-16). Today we know in part, but when Christ comes, we shall know all things as we should know (1 Corinthians 13:12). In the meantime, we continue to look unto Jesus the author and perfecter of our convictions.

BIBLIOGRAPHY

Online encyclopaedia, *Wikipedia*, for definition of various terms and concepts. https://www.wikipedia.com.

Online encyclopaedia, *Britannica*, for definition of various terms. https://www.britannica.com.

Vine's NT Expository Dictionary, for definitions of all Greek words referenced throughout the text. Accessed through https://www.studylight.org.

Welton, J. (2012). *Raptureless* (3rd edn), Kindle version.

END NOTES

INTRODUCTION

[1] 207 people completed my open-invitation "End-time survey," conducted between May 8 – June 12, 2022. 54.6% subscribed to a pre-tribulation catching up of the church; 11.6% leaned towards a mid-tribulation catching up of the church; 5.3% believed in a post-tribulation catching up of the church. Furthermore, 8.2% held no position, and 1.9% believed the Great Tribulation had already occurred.

[2] For this reason, I already envisage and will readily embark on a revision of this work in the future, as and when it becomes necessary.

CHAPTER 1

[1] From the Latin word *praeter*, which means *past*.

CHAPTER 6

[1] Some will argue that this move towards institutionalising the church was itself a tact of the enemy to weaken the spiritual impact of the church, because the church gradually shifted her attention away from the spiritual dynamics of God's kingdom and moved towards outward piety, religiosity, doctrinal errors, and political influence. There were many atrocities attributable to the church that were committed during this time, which persisted throughout the dark ages, until the time of the Reformation.

2 See https://en.wikipedia.org/wiki/Illuminati

CHAPTER 7

1 See https://en.wikipedia.org/wiki/Jacques_Derrida or https://en.wikipedia.org/wiki/Deconstruction

CHAPTER 10

1 For instance, a film, *The Trump Prophecy*, produced in 2018, referred to a word from God received as early as 2011!

2 *Abraham Accords* refers to the normalisation of relations between Israel, USA, and the United Arab Emirates, which also has impacted diplomatic relations with some other Arab nations, including Morocco, Bahrain, and Jordan.

3 North Atlantic Treaty Organisation.

4 World Health Organisation.

5 World Trade Organisation.

DO YOU HAVE COMMENTS, QUESTIONS, OR JUST WANT TO CONNECT WITH THE AUTHOR?

Connect on Facebook:

Omega Word Outreach

Follow on Twitter:

@OmegaWordToks

You Tube:

@OmegaWord

Email:

omegawordoutreach@gmail.com

Website:

www.omegaword.org

Podcast

Omega Word Podcast

ALSO BY TOKUNBO EMMANUEL

Run Church Run

Miracle Shift

The Shift of a Lifetime

The Faith Clinic Revival

The Secret of Abraham

The Wells of Isaac

The Destiny of Jacob

The Mandate of Paul

Marnina: The Woman at the Well

God is Mindful of You

Rediscovering God

Revival in the Desert

The Charismatic Agenda

Sharing the Word of God

A Scribe's Inspiration

Selah Verses

The Glory of Young Men

31 Nuggets of Inspiration

Printed in Great Britain
by Amazon

85645042R00119